TExES
GENERALIST EC-6 191
PRACTICE TEST KIT

By: Sharon Wynne, M.S.

XAMonline, INC.
Boston

Copyright © 2014 XAMonline, Inc.

All rights reserved. No part of the material protected by this copyright notice may be reproduced or utilized in any form or by any means, electronic or mechanical, including photocopying, recording or by any information storage and retrievable system, without written permission from the copyright holder.

To obtain permission(s) to use the material from this work for any purpose including workshops or seminars, please submit a written request to:

XAMonline, Inc.
21 Orient Avenue
Melrose, MA 02176
Toll Free 1-800-509-4128
Email: info@xamonline.com
Web: www.xamonline.com
Fax: 1-617-583-5552

Library of Congress Cataloging-in-Publication Data

Wynne, Sharon A.
    TExES Generalist EC-6 191 Practice Test Kit / Sharon A. Wynne. 1st ed
    ISBN 978-1-60787-396-9
    1. TExES Generalist EC-6 191
    2. Study Guides
    3. TExES
    4. Teachers' Certification & Licensure
    5. Careers

Disclaimer:

The opinions expressed in this publication are the sole works of XAMonline and were created independently from the National Education Association, Educational Testing Service, or any State Department of Education, National Evaluation Systems or other testing affiliates.

Between the time of publication and printing, state specific standards as well as testing formats and Web site information may change and therefore would not be included in part or in whole within this product. Sample test questions are developed by XAMonline and reflect content similar to that on real tests; however, they are not former test questions. XAMonline assembles content that aligns with state standards but makes no claims nor guarantees teacher candidates a passing score. Numerical scores are determined by testing companies such as NES or ETS and then are compared with individual state standards. A passing score varies from state to state.

Printed in the United States of America

TExES Generalist EC-6 191 Practice Test Kit
ISBN: 978-1-60787-396-9

PRETEST

English Language Arts and Reading

(Average) (Skill 1.6)

1. To make a prediction a reader must:

    A. Use text clues to evaluate the text at an inferential level

    B. Find a line of reasoning on which to rely

    C. Make a decision based on an observation

    D. Use prior knowledge and apply it to the current situation

(Average) (Skill 1.10)

2. Which of the following is NOT a characteristic of a good reader?

    A. When faced with unfamiliar words, they skip over them unless meaning is lost

    B. They formulate questions that they predict will be answered in the text

    C. They establish a purpose before reading

    D. They go back to reread when something doesn't make sense

(Rigorous) (Skill 2.1)

3. All of the following are true about schemata EXCEPT:

    A. Used as a basis for literary response

    B. Structures that represent concepts stored in our memories

    C. A generalization that is proven with facts

    D. Used together with prior knowledge for effective reading comprehension

(Average) (Skill 2.2)

4. Children are taught phonological awareness when they are taught all but which concept?

    A. The sounds made by the letters

    B. The correct spelling of words

    C. The sounds made by various combinations of letters

    D. The ability to recognize individual sounds in words

(Average) (Skill 5.4)

5. Which of the following is true about semantics?

    A. Semantics will sharpen the effect and meaning of a text

    B. Semantics refers to the meaning expressed when words are arranged in a specific way

    C. Semantics is a vocabulary instruction technique

    D. Semantics is representing spoken language through the use of symbols

(Average) (Skill 5.5)

6. Spelling instruction should include:

    A. Breaking down sentences

    B. Developing a sense of correct and incorrect spellings

    C. Identifying every word in a given text

    D. Spelling words the way that they sound

(Average) (Skill 6.1)

7. Which of the following reading strategies is NOT associated with fluent reading abilities?

   A. Pronouncing unfamiliar words by finding similarities with familiar words
   B. Establishing a purpose for reading
   C. Formulating questions about the text while reading
   D. Reading sentences word by word

(Rigorous) (Skill 6.3)

8. Mrs. Young is a first grade teacher trying to select a books that are "just right" for her students to read independently. She needs to consider which of the following:

   A. Illustrations should support the meaning of the text.
   B. Content that relates to student interest and experiences
   C. Predictable text structures and language patterns
   D. All of the above

(Average) (Skill 7.5)

9. Answering questions, monitoring comprehension, and interacting with a text are common methods of:

   A. Whole-class instruction
   B. Comprehension instruction
   C. Research-based instruction
   D. Evidence-based instruction

(Average) (Skill 7.11)

10. Which of the following is NOT characteristic of a folktale?

    A. Considered true among various societies
    B. A hero on a quest
    C. Good versus evil
    D. Adventures of animals

(Rigorous) (Skill 7.3)

11. Which of the following did NOT contribute to a separate literature genre for adolescents?

    A. The social changes of post–World War II
    B. The Civil Rights movement
    C. An interest in fantasy and science fiction
    D. Issues surrounding teen pregnancy

(Rigorous) (Skill 7.6)

12. Which of the following is important in understanding fiction?

    I. Realizing the artistry in telling a story to convey a point.
    II. Knowing fiction is imaginary.
    III. Seeing what is truth and what is perspective.
    IV. Acknowledging the difference between opinion and truth.

    A. I and II only
    B. II and IV only
    C. III and IV only
    D. IV only

(Easy) (Skill 4.6)

13. Assonance is a poetic device where:

    A. The vowel sound in a word matches the same sound in a nearby word, but the surrounding consonant sounds are different

    B. The initial sounds of a word, beginning either with a consonant or a vowel, are repeated in close succession

    C. The words used evoke meaning by their sounds

    D. The final consonant sounds are the same, but the vowels are different

(Rigorous) (Skill 4.5)

14. Which of the following is true of the visible shape of poetry?

    I. Forced sound repetition may underscore the meaning.

    II. It was a new rule of poetry after poets began to feel constricted by rhyming conventions.

    III. The shaped reflected the poem's theme.

    IV. It was viewed as a demonstration of ingenuity.

    A. I and II only

    B. II and IV only

    C. III and IV only

    D. IV only

(Average) (Skill 4.2)

15. "Reading maketh a full man, conference a ready man, and writing an exact man" is an example of which type of figurative language?

    A. Euphemism

    B. Bathos

    C. Parallelism

    D. Irony

(Rigorous) (Skill 7.1)

16. Which of the following is NOT a strategy of teaching reading comprehension?

    A. Summarization

    B. Utilizing graphic organizers

    C. Manipulating sounds

    D. Having students generate questions

(Average) (Skill 9.6)

17. Which of the following sentences contains a subject-verb agreement error?

    A. Both mother and her two sisters were married in a triple ceremony

    B. Neither the hen nor the rooster is likely to be served for dinner

    C. My boss, as well as the company's two personnel directors, have been to Spain

    D. Amanda and the twins are late again

(Rigorous) (Skill 9.3)

18. **Which of the following are punctuated correctly?**

    I. The teacher directed us to compare Faulkner's three symbolic novels *Absalom, Absalom*; *As I Lay Dying*; and *Light in August*.

    II. Three of Faulkner's symbolic novels are: *Absalom, Absalom*; *As I Lay Dying*; and *Light in August*.

    III. The teacher directed us to compare Faulkner's three symbolic novels: *Absalom, Absalom*; *As I Lay Dying*; and *Light in August*.

    IV. Three of Faulkner's symbolic novels are *Absalom, Absalom*; *As I Lay Dying*; and *Light in August*.

    A. I and II only
    B. II and III only
    C. III and IV only
    D. IV only

(Rigorous) (Skill 9.7)

19. **All of the following are true about verb tense EXCEPT:**

    A. Present perfect tense is used to express action or a condition that started in the past and is continued to or completed in the present
    B. Future tense is used to express a condition of future time
    C. Past perfect tense expresses action or a condition that occurred as a precedent to some other action or condition
    D. Future participial tense expresses action that started in the past or present and will conclude at some time in the future

(Rigorous) (Skill 9.8)

20. **Which sentence is NOT correct?**

    A. He ought not to get so angry.
    B. I should of gone to bed.
    C. I had set the table before dinner.
    D. I have lain down.

(Average) (Skill 10.4)

21. **All of the following are true about a descriptive essay EXCEPT:**

    A. Its purpose is to make an experience available through one of the five senses
    B. Its words make it possible for the reader to see with their mind's eye
    C. Its language will move people because of the emotion involved
    D. It is not trying to get anyone to take a certain action

(Rigorous) (Skill 8.1)

22. **A student has written a paper with the following characteristics: written in first person; characters, setting, and plot; some dialogue; events organized in chronological sequence with some flashbacks. In what genre has the student written?**

    A. Expository writing
    B. Narrative writing
    C. Persuasive writing
    D. Descriptive writing

(Easy) (Skill 10.1)

23. **The main idea of a paragraph or story:**

    A. Is what the paragraph or story is about

    B. Indicates what the passage is about

    C. Gives more information about the topic

    D. States the important ideas that the author wants the reader to know about a topic

(Rigorous) (Skill 10.2)

24. **A strong topic sentence will:**

    A. Be phrased as a question.

    B. Always be the first sentence in a paragraph.

    C. Both A and B

    D. Neither A nor B

(Average) (Skill 10.6)

25. **Which of the following is a great way to keep a natural atmosphere when speaking publicly?**

    A. Speak slowly

    B. Maintain a straight, but not stiff, posture

    C. Use friendly gestures

    D. Take a step to the side every once in a while

(Rigorous) (Skill 11.9)

26. **Students returning from a field trip to the local newspaper want to thank their hosts for the guided tour. As their teacher, what form of communication should you encourage them to use?**

    A. Each student will send an e-mail expressing his or her appreciation

    B. As a class, students will create a blog, and each student will write about what they learned

    C. Each student will write a thank you letter that the teacher will fax to the newspaper

    D. Each student will write a thank you note that the teacher will mail to the newspaper.

(Rigorous) (Skill 7.8)

27. **Which of the following skills can help students improve their listening comprehension?**

    I. Tap into prior knowledge.

    II. Look for transitions between ideas.

    III. Ask questions of the speaker.

    IV. Discuss the topic being presented.

    A. I and II only

    B. II and IV only

    C. II and IV only

    D. IV only

(Rigorous) (Skill 7.2)

28. As Ms. Wolmark looks at the mandated vocabulary curriculum for the 3rd grade, she notes that she can opt to teach foreign words and abbreviations which have become part of the English language. She decides:

    A. To forego that since she is not a teacher of foreign language
    B. To teach only foreign words from the native language of her four ELL students
    C. To use the ELL students' native languages as a start for an extensive study of foreign language words
    D. To teach 2-3 foreign language words that are now in English and let it go at that

(Rigorous) (Skill 12.12)

29. Which of the following are good choices for supporting a thesis?

    A. Reasons
    B. Examples
    C. Answer to the question, "why?"
    D. All of the above

Math

(Rigorous) (Skill 13.9)

30. A truck rental company charges $40 per day plus $2.50 per mile. The odometer reading is M miles when a customer rents a truck and m miles when it is returned d days later. Which expression represents the total charge for the rental?

    A. $40d + 2.5M - m$
    B. $40d + 2.5m - M$
    C. $40d + 2.5(M - m)$
    D. $40d + 2.5(m - M)$

(Easy) (Skill 13.1)

31. Using a pattern is an appropriate strategy for which of the following:

    I. Skip counting
    II. Counting backward
    III. Finding doubles

    A. I and II
    B. I and III
    C. II and III
    D. I, II, and III

(Rigorous) (Skill 14.5)

32. The following set of numbers is not closed under addition:

    A. Set of all real numbers
    B. Set of all even numbers
    C. Set of all odd numbers
    D. Set of all rational numbers

(Rigorous) (Skill 14.3)

33. What is the value of the following expression?

    $$\frac{5 - 2(6 - 2 \cdot 3)}{-5(2 + 2 \cdot 4)}$$

    A. 0.5

    B. 5.0

    C. -0.5

    D. 3.4

(Average) (Skill 14.4)

34. Which of the following expressions are equivalent to $28 - 4 \cdot 6 + 12$?

    I. $(28 - 4) \cdot 6 + 12$

    II. $28 - (4 \cdot 6) + 12$

    III. $(28 - 4) \cdot (6 + 12)$

    IV. $(28 + 12) - (4 \cdot 6)$

    V. $28 - 4 \cdot 12 + 6$

    A. I and V

    B. II and IV

    C. III and V

    D. IV and V

(Average) (Skill 15.1)

35. If n represents an odd number, which of the following does not represent an even number?

    A. $2n$

    B. $2(n + 1)$

    C. n^2

    D. $10n - 2$

(Rigorous) (Skill 15.5)

36. Based upon the following examples, can you conclude that the sum of two prime numbers is also a prime number? Why or why not?

    $2 + 3 = 5$

    $2 + 5 = 7$

    $11 + 2 = 13$

    A. Yes; there is a pattern

    B. Yes; there are many more examples, such as $17 + 2 = 19$ and $29 + 2 = 31$

    C. No; there are many counterexamples

    D. No; the sums are not prime numbers

(Rigorous) (Skill 15.6)

37. If x is a whole number, what is the best description of the number $4x + 1$?

    A. Prime number

    B. Composite number

    C. Odd number

    D. Even number

(Rigorous) (Skill 15.8)

38. The plot for a proposed new city hall plaza is 120 feet long by 90 feet wide. A scale model for the plaza must fit in an area that is 10 feet square. If the largest possible model is built in that area, what will be the maximum possible width for the scale model?

    A. $\frac{2}{15}$ ft

    B. $1\frac{1}{3}$ ft

    C. $7\frac{1}{2}$ ft

    D. $13\frac{1}{3}$ ft

(Easy) (Skill 17.2)

39. Jocelyn wants create a magnetic board in the back of her classroom by covering part of the wall with a special magnetic paint. Each can of paint will cover 15 square feet. If the area is 12 feet wide and 8 feet high, how many cans of paint should she buy?

   A. 5 cans
   B. 6 cans
   C. 7 cans
   D. 8 cans

(Easy) (Skill 15.3)

40. A recipe makes 6 servings and calls for $1\frac{1}{2}$ cups of rice. How much rice is needed to make 10 servings?

   A. 2 cups
   B. $2\frac{1}{4}$ cups
   C. $2\frac{1}{2}$ cups
   D. $2\frac{3}{4}$ cups

(Rigorous) (Skill 15.10)

41. Which table(s) represents solutions of the following equation?

   I.
x	-5	0	5	10
y	-12	-10	-8	-6

   II.
x	-5	0	5	-10
y	-12	-10	-12	-10

   III.
x	20	25	30	35
y	-2	0	2	4

   A. I
   B. II
   C. II and III
   D. I and III

(Average) (Skill 18.7)

42. The relations given below demonstrate the following addition and multiplication property of real numbers:

   $a + b = b + a$

   $ab = ba$

   A. Commutative
   B. Associative
   C. Identity
   D. Inverse

(Rigorous) (Skill 15.4)

43. Which property (or properties) is applied below?

   $-8x + 5x = (-8 + 5)x$
   $= -3x$

   I. Associative Property of Addition
   II. Zero Property of Addition
   III. Additive Inverses
   IV. Identity Property of Multiplication
   V. Distributive Property

   A. I
   B. V
   C. I and III
   D. II and IV

(Rigorous) (Skill 15.2)

44. For which of the following is the additive inverse equal to the multiplicative inverse?

   A. $\frac{2}{3} + \frac{3}{2}$
   B. $\sqrt{-1}$
   C. $\frac{1 - \sqrt{2}}{1 + \sqrt{2}}$
   D. $(a + b) \div (b - a)$

(Rigorous) (Skill 14.2)

45. Which of the statements below explain the error(s), if any, in the following calculation?

    $\frac{18}{18} + 23 = 23$

    I. A number divided by itself is 1, not 0.

    II. The sum of 1 and 23 is 24, not 23.

    III. The 18s are "cancelled" and replaced by 0.

    A. I and II
    B. II and III
    C. I, II, and III
    D. There is no error.

(Average) (Skill 14.7)

46. Which statement is a model for the following problem?

    27 less than 5 times a number is 193.

    A. $27 < 5x + 193$
    B. $27 - 5x < 193$
    C. $5x - 27 < 193$
    D. $5x - 27 = 193$

(Average) (Skill 14.7)

47. What is the solution set of the following inequality?

    $4x + 9 \geq 11(x - 3)$

    A. $x \leq 0$
    B. $x \geq 0$
    C. $x \leq 6$
    D. $x \geq 6$

(Average) (Skill 13.2)

48. A car is rented in Quebec. The outside temperature shown on the dashboard reads 17°C. What is the temperature in degrees Fahrenheit? (Use the formula $F = \frac{9}{5}C + 32$.)

    A. 27.2°F
    B. 41.4°F
    C. 62.6°F
    D. 88.2°F

(Rigorous) (Skill 15.9)

49. The two solutions of the quadratic equation $ax^2 + bx + c = 0$ are given by the formula

    $x = \frac{-b \pm \sqrt{b^2 - 4ac}}{2a}$.

    What are the solutions of the equation $x^2 - 18x + 32$?

    A. -5 and 23
    B. 2 and 16
    C. $9 \pm \sqrt{113}$
    D. $9 \pm 2\sqrt{113}$

(Rigorous) (Skill 16.2)

50. Triangle *ABC* is rotated 90° clockwise about the origin and translated 6 units left.

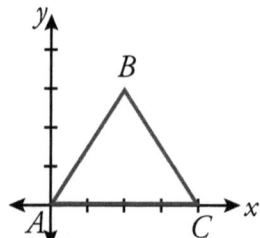

What are the coordinates of *B* after the transformations?

A. (2, −3)
B. (3, −2)
C. (−2, −3)
D. (−3, −2)

(Easy) (Skill 16.1)

51. The following represents the net of a

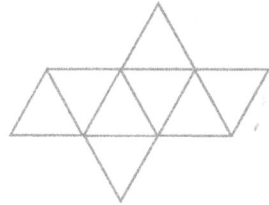

A. Cube
B. Tetrahedron
C. Octahedron
D. Dodecahedron

(Rigorous) (Skill 16.4)

52. Ginny and Nick head back to their respective colleges after being home for the weekend. They leave their house at the same time and drive for 4 hours. Ginny drives due south at the average rate of 60 miles per hour and Nick drives due east at the average rate of 60 miles per hour. What is the straight-line distance between them, in miles, at the end of the 4 hours?

A. 169.7 miles
B. 240 miles
C. 288 miles
D. 339.4 miles

(Rigorous) (Skill 16.3)

53. What is the surface area of the prism shown below?

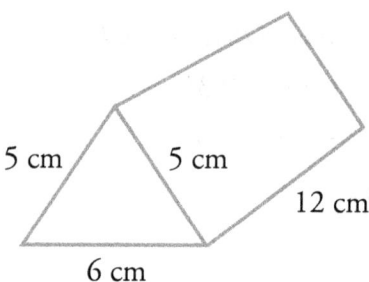

A. 204 cm²
B. 216 cm²
C. 360 cm²
D. 180 cm²

(Rigorous) (Skill 16.6)

54. Find the area of a rectangle if you know that the base is 8 cm and the diagonal of the rectangle is 8.5 cm:

    A. 24 cm²

    B. 30 cm²

    C. 18.9 cm²

    D. 24 cm

(Average) (Skill 16.11)

55. Which of the following is not equivalent to 3 km?

    I. 3.0×10^3 m

    II. 3.0×10^4 cm

    III. 3.0×10^6 mm

    A. I

    B. II

    C. III

    D. None of the above

(Average) (Skill 18.9)

56. A school band has 200 members. Looking at the pie chart below, determine which statement is true about the band.

    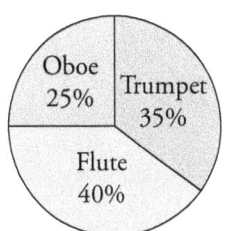

    A. There are more trumpet players than flute players

    B. There are fifty oboe players in the band

    C. There are forty flute players in the band

    D. One-third of all band members play the trumpet

(Rigorous) (Skill 18.5)

57. A restaurant offers the following menu choices.

Green Vegetable	Yellow Vegetable
Asparagus	Carrots
Broccoli	Corn
Peas	Squash
Spinach	

    If a customer chooses a green vegetable and a yellow vegetable at random, what is the probability that the customer will order neither asparagus nor corn?

    A. $\frac{1}{12}$

    B. $\frac{1}{6}$

    C. $\frac{1}{3}$

    D. $\frac{1}{2}$

(Rigorous) (Skill 17.4)

58. Given a drawer with 5 black socks, 3 blue socks, and 2 red socks, what is the probability that you will draw two black socks in two draws in a dark room?

    A. $\frac{2}{9}$

    B. $\frac{1}{4}$

    C. $\frac{17}{18}$

    D. $\frac{1}{18}$

(Rigorous) (Skill 18.3)

59. Find the inverse of the following statement: If I like dogs, then I do not like cats.

    A. If I like dogs, then I do like cats.

    B. If I like cats, then I like dogs.

    C. If I like cats, then I do not like dogs.

    D. If I do not like dogs, then I like cats.

(Average) (Skill 18.6)

60. A school has 15 male teachers and 35 female teachers. In how many ways can they form a committee with 2 male teachers and 4 female teachers on it?

    A. 525

    B. 5497800

    C. 88

    D. 263894400

(Rigorous) (Skill 18.8)

61. A music store owner wants to change the window display every week. Only 4 out of 6 instruments can be displayed in the window at the same time. How many weeks will it be before the owner must repeat the same arrangement (in the same order) of instruments in the window display?

    A. 24 weeks

    B. 36 weeks

    C. 120 weeks

    D. 360 weeks

(Rigorous) (Skill 18.2)

62. Half the students in a class scored 80% on an exam; one student scored 10%; and the rest of the class scored 85%. Which would be the best measure of central tendency for the test scores?

    A. Mean

    B. Median

    C. Mode

    D. Either the median or the mode because they are equal

SOCIAL SCIENCES

(Average) (Skill 21.1)

63. The Great Plains in the United States are an excellent place to grow corn and wheat for all of the following reasons EXCEPT:

    A. Rainfall is abundant and the soil is rich

    B. The land is mostly flat and easy to cultivate

    C. The human population is modest in size, so there is plenty of space for large farms

    D. The climate is semitropical

(Easy) (Skill 19.11)

64. Ms. Gomez has a number of ESOL students in her class. In order to meet their specific needs as second-language learners, which of the following would NOT be an appropriate approach?

    A. Pair students of different ability levels for English practice

    B. Focus most of her instruction on teaching English rather than content

    C. Provide accommodations during testing and with assignments

    D. Use visual aids to help students make word links with familiar objects

(Average) (Skill 22.8)

65. In the 1800s, the era of industrialization and growth was characterized by:

    A. Small firms

    B. Public ownership

    C. Worker-owned enterprises

    D. Monopolies and trusts

(Rigorous) (Skill 21.22)

66. What is characteristic of areas of the world with high populations?

    A. These areas tend to have heavy pollution

    B. These areas are almost always surrounded by suburbs

    C. Populations are rarely located near one another

    D. Most populated places in the world also tend to be close to agricultural lands

(Average) (Skill 22.8)

67. In the 1800s, the era of industrialization and growth was characterized by:

    A. Small firms

    B. Public ownership

    C. Worker-owned enterprises

    D. Monopolies and trusts

(Average) (Skill 21.20)

68. Meridians, or lines of longitude, not only help in pinpointing locations but are also used for:

    A. Measuring distance from the Poles

    B. Determining direction of ocean currents

    C. Determining the time around the world

    D. Measuring distance on the equator

(Rigorous) (Skill 21.16)

69. The Western Hemisphere contains all of which of the following continents?

    A. Russia
    B. Europe
    C. North America
    D. Asia

(Rigorous) (Skill 21.19)

70. Mr. Allen is discussing the earthquake in Chile and explains the aftershocks and tsunamis that threatened Pacific islands thousands of miles away. What aspect of geographical studies was he emphasizing?

    A. Regional
    B. Topical
    C. Physical
    D. Human

(Average) (Skill 21.11)

71. Which of the following are non-renewable resources?

    A. Fish, coffee, and forests
    B. Fruit, water, and solar energy
    C. Wind power, alcohol, and sugar
    D. Coal, natural gas, and oil

(Average) (Skill 21.23)

72. What people perfected the preservation of dead bodies?

    A. Sumerians
    B. Phoenicians
    C. Egyptians
    D. Assyrians

(Rigorous) (Skill 21.9)

73. Which of these is NOT a true statement about the Roman civilization?

    A. Its period of Pax Romana provided long periods of peace during which travel and trade increased, enabling the spread of culture, goods, and ideas over the known world
    B. It borrowed the concept of democracy from the Greeks and developed it into a complex representative government
    C. It flourished in the arts with a realistic approach to art and a dramatic use of architecture
    D. It developed agricultural innovations such as crop rotation and terrace farming

(Average) (Skill 23.6)

74. The major force in eighteenth and nineteenth century politics was:

    A. Nationalism
    B. Revolution
    C. War
    D. Diplomacy

(Average) (Skill 21.14)

75. The identification of individuals or groups as they are influenced by their own group or culture is called:

    A. Cross-cultural exchanges
    B. Cultural diffusion
    C. Cultural identity
    D. Cosmopolitanism

(Average) (Skill 20.24)

76. The New England colonies included:

    A. South Carolina
    B. Georgia
    C. Massachusetts
    D. New York

(Rigorous) (Skill 20.22)

77. Which major economic activity of the Southern colonies led to the growth of slavery?

    A. Manufacturing
    B. Fishing
    C. Farming
    D. Coal mining

(Average) (Skill 20.18)

78. Which was the first instance of an internal tax on the American colonies?

    A. The Proclamation Act
    B. The Sugar Act
    C. The Currency Act
    D. The Stamp Act

(Average) (Skill 20.19)

79. The Lewis and Clark expedition advanced knowledge in each of the following areas EXCEPT:

    A. Geography
    B. Modern warfare
    C. Botany
    D. Animal life

(Average) (Skill 20.23)

80. Populism arises out of a feeling:

    A. Of intense happiness
    B. Of satisfaction with the activities of large corporations
    C. That women should not be allowed to vote
    D. Perceived oppression

(Average) (Skill 20.16)

81. At the end of the Twentieth Century, the United States was:

    A. A central leader in international affairs
    B. A reluctant participant in international affairs
    C. One of two superpowers
    D. Lacking a large consumer culture

(Rigorous) (Skill 20.17)

82. How did manufacturing change in the early 1800s?

    A. The electronics industry was born
    B. Production moved from small shops or homes into factories
    C. Industry benefited from the Federal Reserve Act
    D. The timber industry was hurt when Theodore Roosevelt set aside 238 million acres of federal lands to be protected from development

(Rigorous) (Skill 22.7)

83. The early ancient civilizations developed systems of government:

    A. To provide for defense against attack
    B. To regulate trade
    C. To regulate and direct the economic activities of the people as they worked together in groups
    D. To decide on the boundaries of the different fields during planting seasons

(Rigorous) (Skill 20.1)

84. What is another name for dictatorship?

    A. Oligarchy
    B. Monarchy
    C. Anarchism
    D. Communism

(Average) (Skill 23.3)

85. Which of the following documents described and defined the system and structure of the United States government?

    A. The Bill of Rights
    B. The Declaration of Independence
    C. The Constitution
    D. The Articles of Confederation

(Rigorous) (Skill 23.4)

86. How did the ideology of John Locke influence Thomas Jefferson in writing the Declaration of Independence?

    A. Locke emphasized human rights and believed that people should rebel against governments who violated those rights
    B. Locke emphasized the rights of government to protect its people and to levy taxes
    C. Locke believed in the British system of monarchy and the rights of Parliament to make laws
    D. Locke advocated individual rights over the collective whole

(Average) (Skill 23.1)

87. Which of the following is not a right declared by the U.S. Constitution?

    A. The right to speak out in public
    B. The right to use cruel and unusual punishment
    C. The right to a speedy trial
    D. The right not to be forced to testify against yourself

(Rigorous) (Skill 22.5)

88. The cold weather froze orange crops in Florida and the price of orange juice increased. This is an example of what economic concept?

    A. Output market
    B. Input market
    C. Supply and demand
    D. Entrepreneurship

(Average) (Skill 22.4)

89. What type of production process must producers choose?

   A. One that is inefficient
   B. One that often produces goods that consumers don't want
   C. One that is efficient
   D. One that is sometimes efficient and sometimes inefficient

(Rigorous) (Skill 22.6)

90. The existence of economics is based on:

   A. The scarcity of resources
   B. The abundance of resources
   C. Little or nothing that is related to resources
   D. Entrepreneurship

(Rigorous) (Skill 22.2)

91. In the fictional country of Nacirema, the government controls the means of production and directs resources. It alone decides what will be produced; as a result, there is an abundance of capital and military goods but a scarcity of consumer goods. What type of economy is this?

   A. Market economy
   B. Centrally planned economy
   C. Market socialism
   D. Capitalism

(Average) (Skill 19.8)

92. Which of the following are secondary research materials?

   A. The conclusions and inferences of other historians
   B. Literature and nonverbal materials, novels, stories, poetry, and essays from the period, as well as coins, archaeological artifacts, and art produced during the period
   C. Interviews and surveys conducted by the researcher
   D. Statistics gathered as the result of the research's experiments

(Rigorous) (Skill 19.6)

93. For their research paper on the effects of the Civil War on American literature, students have brainstormed a list of potential online sources and are seeking your authorization. Which of these represent the strongest source?

   A. http://www.wikipedia.org/
   B. http://www.google.com
   C. http://www.nytimes.com
   D. http://docsouth.unc.edu/southlit/civilwar.html

(Rigorous) (Skill 19.7)

94. For the historian studying ancient Egypt, which of the following would be least useful?

   A. The record of an ancient Greek historian on Greek-Egyptian interaction
   B. Letters from an Egyptian ruler to his/her regional governors
   C. Inscriptions on stele of the Fourteenth Egyptian Dynasty
   D. Letters from a nineteenth century Egyptologist to his wife

(Rigorous) (Skill 19.1)

95. Which of the following can be considered the primary goal of social studies?

   A. Recalling specific dates and places
   B. Identifying and analyzing social links
   C. Using contextual clues to identify eras
   D. Linking experiments with history

SCIENCE

(Easy) (Skill 38.1)

96. Which is the correct order for the layers of Earth's atmosphere?

   A. Troposphere, stratosphere, mesosphere, and thermosphere
   B. Mesosphere, stratosphere, troposphere, and thermosphere
   C. Troposphere, stratosphere, thermosphere, and mesosphere
   D. Thermosphere, troposphere, stratosphere, mesosphere

(Rigorous) (Skill 34.2)

97. What kind of chemical reaction is photosynthesis?

   A. Fusion
   B. Exothermic
   C. Endothermic
   D. Could be exothermic or endothermic

(Easy) (Skill 39.1)

98. What type of rock can be classified by the size of the crystals in the rock?

   A. Metamorphic
   B. Igneous
   C. Minerals
   D. Sedimentary

(Easy) (Skill 36.2)

99. In which of the following eras did life appear?

   A. Paleozoic
   B. Mesozoic
   C. Cenozoic
   D. Precambrian

(Easy) (Skill 39.5)

100. The use of radioactivity to determine the age of rocks and fossils is called which of the following?

   A. Carbon dating
   B. Absolute dating
   C. Stratigraphy
   D. Geological dating

(Easy) (Skill 41.1)

101. Which of the following astronomical entities is not part of the galaxy the Sun is located in?

   A. Nebulae
   B. Quasars
   C. Pulsars
   D. Neutron stars

(Average) (Skill 41.2)

102. Why is the winter in the southern hemisphere colder than winter in the northern hemisphere?

   A. Earth's axis of 24-hour rotation tilts at an angle of $23\frac{1}{2}$
   B. The elliptical orbit of Earth around the Sun changes the distance of the Sun from Earth
   C. The southern hemisphere has more water than the northern hemisphere
   D. The green house effect is greater for the northern hemisphere

(Average) (Skill 34.1)

103. Which of the following is not a property that eukaryotes have and prokaryotes do not have?

   A. Nucleus
   B. Ribosomes
   C. Chromosomes
   D. Mitochondria

(Easy) (Skill 34.4)

104. Which of the following processes and packages macromolecules?

   A. Lysosomes
   B. Cytosol
   C. Golgi apparatus
   D. Plastids

(Easy) (Skill 35.1)

105. Which is not a characteristic of living organisms?

   A. Sexual reproduction
   B. Ingestion
   C. Synthesis
   D. Respiration

(Average) (Skill 35.3)

106. At what stage in mitosis does the chromatin become chromosomes?

   A. Telophase
   B. Anaphase
   C. Prophase
   D. Metaphase

(Average) (Skill 36.1)

107. Which of the following is not part of Darwinian evolution?

   A. Survival of the fittest
   B. Random mutations
   C. Heritability of acquired traits
   D. Natural selection

(Easy) (Skill 37.3)

108. Taxonomy classifies species into genera (plural of genus) based on similarities. Species are subordinate to genera. The most general or highest taxonomical group is the kingdom. Which of the following is the correct order of the other groups from highest to lowest?

   A. Class ⇒ order ⇒ family ⇒ phylum
   B. Phylum ⇒ class ⇒ family ⇒ order
   C. Phylum ⇒ class ⇒ order ⇒ family
   D. Order ⇒ phylum ⇒ class ⇒ family

(Easy) (Skill 36.3)

109. Which of the following describes the interaction between community members when one species feeds of another species but does not kill it immediately?

   A. Parasitism
   B. Predation
   C. Commensalism
   D. Mutualism

(Easy) (Skill 31.3)

110. Which of the following statements about the density of a substance is true?

   A. It is a chemical property
   B. It is a physical property
   C. It does not depend on the temperature of the substance
   D. It is a property only of liquids and solids

(Easy) (Skill 31.1)

111. The electrons in a neutral atom that is not in an excited energy state are in various energy shells. For example, there are two electrons in the lowest energy shell and eight in the next shell if the atom contains more than 10 electrons. How many electrons are in the shell with the maximum number of electrons?

   A. 8
   B. 18
   C. 32
   D. 44

(Rigorous) (Skill 27.1)

112. Which statement best explains why a balance scale is used to measure both weight and mass?

   A. The weight and mass of an object are identical concepts
   B. The force of gravity between two objects depends on the mass of the two objects
   C. Inertial mass and gravitational mass are identical
   D. A balance scale compares the weight of two objects

(Average) (Skill 30.3)

113. Which of the following does not determine the frictional force between a box sliding down a ramp?

   A. The weight of the box
   B. The area of the box
   C. The angle the ramp makes with the horizontal
   D. The chemical properties of the two surfaces

(Easy) (Skill 40.1)

114. Which statement is true about temperature?

   A. Temperature is a measurement of heat
   B. Temperature is how hot or cold an object is
   C. The coldest temperature ever measured is zero degrees Kelvin
   D. The temperature of a molecule is its kinetic energy

(Rigorous) (Skill 32.2)

115. When glass is heated, it becomes softer and softer until it becomes a liquid. Which of the following statements best describes this phenomenon?

   A. Glass has no heat of vaporization

   B. Glass has no heat of fusion

   C. The latent heat of glass is zero calories per gram

   D. Glass is made up of crystals

(Average) (Skill 32.1)

116. Which statement could be described as the first law of thermodynamics?

   A. No machine can convert heat energy to work with 100 percent efficiency

   B. Energy is neither created nor destroyed

   C. Thermometers can be used to measure temperatures

   D. Heat flows from hot objects to cold objects

(Average) (Skill 31.6)

117. What kind of chemical reaction is the burning of coal?

   A. Exothermic and composition

   B. Exothermic and decomposition

   C. Endothermic and composition

   D. Endothermic and decomposition

(Easy) (Skill 33.3)

118. Which of the following is a result of a nuclear reaction called fission?

   A. Sunlight

   B. Cosmic radiation

   C. Supernova

   D. Existence of the elements in the periodic table

(Easy) (Skill 25.3)

119. What is technology?

   A. The application of science to satisfy human needs

   B. Knowledge of complex machines, computer systems, and manufacturing processes

   C. The study of engineering

   D. A branch of science

(Average) (Skill 28.2)

120. An experiment is performed to determine how the surface area of a liquid affects how long it takes for the liquid to evaporate. One hundred milliliters of water is put in containers with surface areas of 10 cm², 30 cm², 50 cm², 70 cm², and 90 cm². The time it took for each container to evaporate is recorded. Which of the following is a controlled variable?

   A. The time required for each evaporation

   B. The area of the surfaces

   C. The amount of water

   D. The temperature of the water

(Rigorous) (Skill 28.8)

121. Stars near Earth can be seen to move relative to fixed stars. In observing the motion of a nearby star over a period of decades, an astronomer notices that the path is not a straight line but wobbles about a straight line. The astronomer reports in a peer-reviewed journal that a planet is rotating around the star, causing it to wobble. Which of the following statements best describes the proposition that the star has a planet?

    A. Observation
    B. Hypothesis
    C. Theory
    D. Inference

THE ARTS, HEALTH AND PHYSICAL EDUCATION

(Easy) (Skill 43.4)

122. In order to promote diversity, a teacher should:

    A. Introduce a variety of musical genres
    B. Allow students to experiment with all different musical instruments
    C. Expose students to various composers
    D. All of the above

(Average) (Skill 44.1)

123. Calisthenics develops all of the following health and skill related components of fitness except:

    A. Muscle strength
    B. Body composition
    C. Power
    D. Agility

(Average) (Skill 44.12)

124. Playing "Simon Says" and having students touch different body parts applies which movement concept?

    A. Spatial Awareness
    B. Effort Awareness
    C. Body Awareness
    D. Motion Awareness

(Average) (Skill 45.7)

125. What is the proper sequential order of development for the acquisition of nonlocomotor skills?

    A. Stretch, sit, bend, turn, swing, twist, shake, rock & sway, dodge; fall
    B. Bend, stretch, turn, twist, swing, sit, rock & sway, shake, dodge; fall
    C. Stretch, bend, sit, shake, turn, rock & sway, swing, twist, dodge; fall
    D. Bend, stretch, sit, turn, twist, swing, sway, rock & sway, dodge; fall

(Average) (Skill 44.2)

126. Which of these is a type of joint?

    A. Ball and socket
    B. Hinge
    C. Pivot
    D. All of the above

(Average) (Skill 45.4)

127. Which movement concept involves students making decisions about an object's positional changes in space?

    A. Spatial Awareness
    B. Effort Awareness
    C. Body Awareness
    D. Motion Awareness

(Rigorous) (Skill 42.3)

128. **Swimming does not improve which health or skill related component of fitness?**
    - A. Cardio-respiratory function
    - B. Flexibility
    - C. Muscle strength
    - D. Foot Speed

(Average) (Skill 44.14)

129. **The main source of energy comes from?**
    - A. Carbohydrates
    - B. Water
    - C. Protein
    - D. Fats

(Average) (Skill 45.2)

130. **Which one of these will not help assess current fitness levels and progress?**
    - A. Fitnessgram
    - B. Pedometers
    - C. Presidential Fitness Assessments
    - D. Body Mass Index

(Rigorous) (Skill 45.1)

131. **Which is not a benefit of warming up?**
    - A. Releasing hydrogen from myoglobin
    - B. Reducing the risk of musculoskeletal injuries
    - C. Raising the body's core temperature in preparation for activity
    - D. Preparing the body for physical activity

(Average) (Skill 45.11)

132. **In a physical education classroom, the teacher must:**
    - A. Adapt lessons to meet the needs of all learners and included IEP modifications
    - B. Only include short term goals to help the student to succeed
    - C. Expect the regular education teacher to meet each child's developmental needs
    - D. None of the above

(Easy) (Skill 45.12)

133. **Which of the following is not a manipulative skill?**
    - A. Hitting a ball
    - B. Jumping rope
    - C. Juggling
    - D. Skipping

(Easy) (Skill 45.5)

134. **Which of the following is not a category of a movement concept?**
    - A. Spacial awareness
    - B. Body awareness
    - C. Manipulative skills
    - D. Locomotor movements

(Easy) (Skill 43.3)

135. A music teacher plans an end of the year celebration to conclude the school year. The first grade students she is arranging music for will most likely sing songs that are:

    A. Largo

    B. Grave

    C. Vivace

    D. None of the above

(Easy) (Skill 43.3)

136. After demonstrating her knowledge of the piano and discussing her career with her students, Ms. Bellante, a music teacher:

    A. Helps students to understand her role within the school system

    B. Allows students to understand ways in which they may be involved in music

    C. Encourages trying new concepts

    D. All of the above

(Average) (Skill 43.2)

137. A series of single tones that add up to a recognizable sound is called a:

    A. Cadence

    B. Rhythm

    C. Melody

    D. Sequence

(Easy)

138. When planning a production, Mr. Garrett's class begins practicing on the stage. He instructs some of his students to wait quietly off to the side of the stage before their parts begin. The place he is referring to is known as:

    A. Upstage

    B. The wings

    C. The legs

    D. The orchestra pit

(Average)

139. A teacher assigns her students with the task of moving creatively in a way that expresses a given word. This allows students to:

    A. Understand vocabulary words

    B. Demonstrate creative expression and performance

    C. Promote confidence

    D. All of the above

(Easy) (Skill 46.7)

140. An appropriate theatrical production for young students is:

    A. *West Side Story*

    B. *Peter Pan*

    C. *Macbeth*

    D. *The Lost Colony*

Pretest Answer Key

1. A	15. C	29. D	43. B	57. D	71. D	85. C	99. D	113. B	127. A
2. A	16. C	30. D	44. B	58. A	72. C	86. A	100. B	114. B	128. D
3. C	17. C	31. A	45. C	59. D	73. D	87. B	101. B	115. B	129. A
4. B	18. C	32. C	46. D	60. B	74. A	88. C	102. B	116. B	130. D
5. B	19. D	33. C	47. C	61. D	75. C	89. C	103. B	117. A	131. A
6. B	20. B	34. B	48. C	62. B	76. C	90. A	104. C	118. D	132. A
7. D	21. D	35. C	49. B	63. D	77. C	91. B	105. A	119. A	133. D
8. D	22. B	36. C	50. D	64. B	78. D	92. A	106. C	120. C	134. C
9. B	23. D	37. C	51. C	65. D	79. B	93. D	107. C	121. D	135. C
10. A	24. D	38. C	52. D	66. D	80. D	94. D	108. C	122. D	136. D
11. C	25. C	39. C	53. B	67. D	81. A	95. B	109. A	123. C	137. C
12. A	26. D	40. C	54. A	68. C	82. B	96. A	110. B	124. C	138. B
13. A	27. A	41. D	55. B	69. C	83. C	97. D	111. C	125. C	139. D
14. C	28. C	42. A	56. B	70. C	84. A	98. B	112. C	126. D	140. B

Pretest Rigor Table

Easy 20%	13, 23, 31, 39, 40, 64, 96, 98, 99, 100, 101, 104, 105, 108, 109, 110, 111, 114, 118, 119, 122, 133, 134, 135, 136, 138, 140
Average 40%	1, 2, 4, 5, 6, 7, 9, 10, 15, 17, 21, 25, 34, 35, 42, 46, 48, 55, 56, 63, 65, 67, 68, 71, 72, 74, 75, 77, 78, 79, 80, 81, 85, 87, 89, 92, 102, 103, 106, 107, 113, 116, 117, 120, 123, 124, 125, 126, 127, 129, 130, 132, 137, 139
Rigorous 40%	3, 8, 11, 12, 14, 16, 18, 19, 20, 22, 24, 26, 27, 28, 29, 30, 32, 33, 36, 37, 38, 41, 43, 44, 45, 49, 50, 52, 53, 57, 58, 59, 61, 62, 66, 69, 70, 73, 76, 82, 83, 84, 86, 88, 90, 91, 93, 94, 95, 97, 112, 115, 121, 128, 131

PRETEST WITH RATIONALES

English Language Arts and Reading

(Average) (Skill 1.6)

1. **To make a prediction a reader must:**
   A. Use text clues to evaluate the text at an inferential level
   B. Find a line of reasoning on which to rely
   C. Make a decision based on an observation
   D. Use prior knowledge and apply it to the current situation

   Answer: A. Use text clues to evaluate the text at an inferential level.

   Making a prediction requires the reader to evaluate a text by going beyond the literal level of what is stated to an inferential level by using text clues to make predictions as to what will happen next in the text. Because choices B–D do not involve evaluating a text on an inferential level, they are not correct ways to make a prediction.

(Average) (Skill 1.10)

2. **Which of the following is NOT a characteristic of a good reader?**
   A. When faced with unfamiliar words, they skip over them unless meaning is lost
   B. They formulate questions that they predict will be answered in the text
   C. They establish a purpose before reading
   D. They go back to reread when something doesn't make sense

   Answer: A. When faced with unfamiliar words, they skip over them unless meaning is lost

   While skipping over an unknown word may not compromise the meaning of the text, a good reader will attempt to pronounce the word by using analogies to familiar words. They also formulate questions, establish a purpose, and go back to reread if meaning is lost.

(Rigorous) (Skill 2.1)

3. **All of the following are true about schemata EXCEPT:**
   A. Used as a basis for literary response
   B. Structures that represent concepts stored in our memories
   C. A generalization that is proven with facts
   D. Used together with prior knowledge for effective reading comprehension

   Answer: C. A generalization that is proven with facts

   Schemata are structures that represent concepts stored in the memory. When used together with prior knowledge and ideas from the printed text while reading, comprehension takes place. Schemata have nothing to do with making a generalization and proving it with facts.

(Average) (Skill 2.2)

4. **Children are taught phonological awareness when they are taught all but which concept?**

    A. The sounds made by the letters

    B. The correct spelling of words

    C. The sounds made by various combinations of letters

    D. The ability to recognize individual sounds in words

Answer: B. The correct spelling of words.

Phonological awareness happens during the pre-K years or even earlier and involves connecting letters to sounds. Children begin to develop a sense of correct and incorrect spellings of words in a transitional spelling phase that is traditionally entered in elementary school.

(Average) (Skill 5.4)

5. **Which of the following is true about semantics?**

    A. Semantics will sharpen the effect and meaning of a text

    B. Semantics refers to the meaning expressed when words are arranged in a specific way

    C. Semantics is a vocabulary instruction technique

    D. Semantics is representing spoken language through the use of symbols

Answer: B. Semantics refers to the meaning expressed when words are arranged in a specific way

Understanding semantics means understanding that meaning is imbedded in the order of words in a sentence. Changing the order of the words would change the meaning of a sentence. The other three choices do not involve finding meaning through the order of words.

(Average) (Skill 5.5)

6. **Spelling instruction should include:**

    A. Breaking down sentences

    B. Developing a sense of correct and incorrect spellings

    C. Identifying every word in a given text

    D. Spelling words the way that they sound

Answer: B. Developing a sense of correct and incorrect spellings

Developing a sense of correct and incorrect spellings is part of the developmental stages of spelling and is a phase that is typically entered later in elementary school. Breaking down sentences involves paragraph analysis, identifying every word in a given text is not necessary to construct meaning from that text, and spelling words the way that they sound is not an effective way to teach spelling.

(Average) (Skill 6.1)

7. **Which of the following reading strategies is NOT associated with fluent reading abilities?**

    A. Pronouncing unfamiliar words by finding similarities with familiar words

    B. Establishing a purpose for reading

    C. Formulating questions about the text while reading

    D. Reading sentences word by word

Answer: D. Reading sentences word by word

Pronouncing unfamiliar words by finding similarities with familiar words, establishing a purpose for reading, and formulating questions about the text while reading are all strategies fluent readers use to enhance their comprehension of a text. Reading sentences word by word is a trait of a nonfluent reader. It inhibits comprehension, as the reader focuses on each word separately rather than the meaning of the whole sentence and how it fits into the text.

(Rigorous) (Skill 6.3)

8. Mrs. Young is a first grade teacher trying to select a books that are "just right" for her students to read independently. She needs to consider which of the following:

    A. Illustrations should support the meaning of the text.
    B. Content that relates to student interest and experiences
    C. Predictable text structures and language patterns
    D. All of the above

Answer: D. All of the above

It is important that all of the above factors be considered when selecting books for young children.

(Average) (Skill 7.5)

9. Answering questions, monitoring comprehension, and interacting with a text are common methods of:

    A. Whole-class instruction
    B. Comprehension instruction
    C. Research-based instruction
    D. Evidence-based instruction

Answer: B. Comprehension instruction

Comprehension instruction helps students learn strategies that they can use independently with any text. Answering questions, monitoring comprehension, and interacting with a text are a few strategies that teachers can teach to their students to help increase their comprehension. Research-based, evidence-based, and whole-class instruction relate to specific reading programs available.

(Average) (Skill 7.11)

10. Which of the following is NOT characteristic of a folktale?

    A. Considered true among various societies
    B. A hero on a quest
    C. Good versus evil
    D. Adventures of animals

Answer: A. Considered true among various societies

There are few societies that would consider folktales to be true as folktale is another name for fairy tale, and elements such as heroes on a quest, good versus evil, and adventures of animals are popular, fictional, themes in fairy tales.

(Rigorous) (Skill 7.3)

11. **Which of the following did NOT contribute to a separate literature genre for adolescents?**

    A. The social changes of post–World War II

    B. The Civil Rights movement

    C. An interest in fantasy and science fiction

    D. Issues surrounding teen pregnancy

Answer: C. An interest in fantasy and science fiction

Social changes after World War II, the Civil Rights movement, and personal issues like teen pregnancy all contributed to authors writing a new breed of contemporary fiction to help adolescents understand and cope with the world they live in. Adolescents may be interested in fantasy and science fiction topics but that interest did not cause the creation of an entire genre.

(Rigorous) (Skill 7.6)

12. **Which of the following is important in understanding fiction?**

    I. Realizing the artistry in telling a story to convey a point.

    II. Knowing fiction is imaginary.

    III. Seeing what is truth and what is perspective.

    IV. Acknowledging the difference between opinion and truth.

    A. I and II only

    B. II and IV only

    C. III and IV only

    D. IV only

Answer: A. I and II only

In order to understand a piece of fiction, it is important that readers realize that an author's choice in a work of fiction is for the sole purpose of conveying a viewpoint. It is also important to understand that fiction is imaginary. Seeing what is truth and what is perspective and acknowledging the difference between opinion and truth are important in understanding nonfiction.

(Easy) (Skill 4.6)

13. **Assonance is a poetic device where:**

    A. The vowel sound in a word matches the same sound in a nearby word, but the surrounding consonant sounds are different

    B. The initial sounds of a word, beginning either with a consonant or a vowel, are repeated in close succession

    C. The words used evoke meaning by their sounds

    D. The final consonant sounds are the same, but the vowels are different

Answer: A. The vowel sound in a word matches the same sound in a nearby word, but the surrounding consonant sounds are different

Assonance takes the middle territory of rhyming so that the vowel sounds are similar, but the consonant sounds are different: "tune" and "food" are assonant. Repeating words in close succession that have the same initial sound ("puppies who pant pathetically") is alliteration. Using the sounds of words to evoke meaning ("zip, pow, pop") is onomatopoeia. When final consonant sounds are the same and the vowels are different, and author has used a different kind of alliteration.

(Rigorous) (Skill 4.5)

14. Which of the following is true of the visible shape of poetry?

    I. Forced sound repetition may underscore the meaning.
    II. It was a new rule of poetry after poets began to feel constricted by rhyming conventions.
    III. The shaped reflected the poem's theme.
    IV. It was viewed as a demonstration of ingenuity.

    A. I and II only
    B. II and IV only
    C. III and IV only
    D. IV only

Answer: C. III and IV only

During the seventeenth century, some poets shaped their poems on the page. The shape would reflect the poem's theme. While an interesting device, the skill was viewed as a demonstration of ingenuity but did not add to the effect or meaning of the poem. Sound repetition has no effect on the visible shape of a poem. Shaping a poem was never a rule all poets deemed to follow.

(Average) (Skill 4.2)

15. "Reading maketh a full man, conference a ready man, and writing an exact man" is an example of which type of figurative language?

    A. Euphemism
    B. Bathos
    C. Parallelism
    D. Irony

Answer: C. Parallelism

Parallelism is the arrangement of ideas into phrases, sentences, and paragraphs that balance one element with another of equal importance and similar wording. In the example given, reading, conference, and writing are balanced in importance and wording. A euphemism substitutes an agreeable term for one that might offend. Bathos is a ludicrous attempt to evoke pity, sympathy, or sorrow. Irony is using an expression that is the opposite to the literal meaning.

(Rigorous) (Skill 7.1)

16. Which of the following is NOT a strategy of teaching reading comprehension?

    A. Summarization
    B. Utilizing graphic organizers
    C. Manipulating sounds
    D. Having students generate questions

Answer: C. Manipulating sounds

Comprehension simply means that the reader can ascribe meaning to text. Teachers can use many strategies to teach comprehension, including questioning, asking students to paraphrase or summarize, utilizing graphic organizers, and focusing on mental images.

(Average) (Skill 9.6)

17. Which of the following sentences contains a subject-verb agreement error?

    A. Both mother and her two sisters were married in a triple ceremony
    B. Neither the hen nor the rooster is likely to be served for dinner

C. My boss, as well as the company's two personnel directors, have been to Spain

D. Amanda and the twins are late again

Answer: C. My boss, as well as the company's two personnel directors, have been to Spain

In choice C, the true subject of the verb is "My boss," not "two personnel directors." Because the subject is singular, the verb form must be singular, "has." In choices A and D, the compound subjects are joined by "and" and take the plural form of the verb. In choice B, the compound subject is joined by "nor" so the verb must agree with the subject closer to the verb. "Rooster" is singular so the correct verb is "is."

(Rigorous) (Skill 9.3)

18. **Which of the following are punctuated correctly?**

    I. The teacher directed us to compare Faulkner's three symbolic novels *Absalom, Absalom*; *As I Lay Dying*; and *Light in August*.

    II. Three of Faulkner's symbolic novels are: *Absalom, Absalom*; *As I Lay Dying*; and *Light in August*.

    III. The teacher directed us to compare Faulkner's three symbolic novels: *Absalom, Absalom*; *As I Lay Dying*; and *Light in August*.

    IV. Three of Faulkner's symbolic novels are *Absalom, Absalom*; *As I Lay Dying*; and *Light in August*.

    A. I and II only

    B. II and III only

    C. III and IV only

    D. IV only

Answer: C. III and IV only

These sentences are focusing on the use of a colon. The rule is to place a colon at the beginning of a list of items except when the list is preceded by a verb. Sentences I and III do not have a verb before the list and therefore need a colon. Sentences II and IV have a verb before the list and therefore do not need a colon.

(Rigorous) (Skill 9.7)

19. **All of the following are true about verb tense EXCEPT:**

    A. Present perfect tense is used to express action or a condition that started in the past and is continued to or completed in the present

    B. Future tense is used to express a condition of future time

    C. Past perfect tense expresses action or a condition that occurred as a precedent to some other action or condition

    D. Future participial tense expresses action that started in the past or present and will conclude at some time in the future

Answer: D. Future participial tense expresses action that started in the past or present and will conclude at some time in the future

Choices A–C are correct statements about each type of verb tense. D is incorrect because there is no such thing as future participial tense.

(Rigorous) (Skill 9.8)

20. **Which sentence is NOT correct?**

    A. He ought not to get so angry.

    B. I should of gone to bed.

    C. I had set the table before dinner.

    D. I have lain down.

Answer: B. I should of gone to bed.

The most frequent problems in verb use come from the improper formation of the past and past participial forms. Choices A, C, and D may sound awkward but are actually correct uses of the participial tense. "I should of gone to bed" is incorrect because "of" is not a verb. A correct sentence would be, "I should have gone to bed."

(Average) (Skill 10.4)

21. **All of the following are true about a descriptive essay EXCEPT:**

    A. Its purpose is to make an experience available through one of the five senses

    B. Its words make it possible for the reader to see with their mind's eye

    C. Its language will move people because of the emotion involved

    D. It is not trying to get anyone to take a certain action

Answer: D. It is not trying to get anyone to take a certain action

The descriptive essay uses language to make an experience available to readers. It uses descriptive words so the reader can see with their mind's eye, smell with their mind's nose, etc. Descriptive writing will involve the emotions of both the reader and writer. Poems are excellent examples of descriptive writing. An exposition is the type of essay that is not interested in getting anyone to take a certain action.

(Rigorous) (Skill 8.1)

22. **A student has written a paper with the following characteristics: written in first person; characters, setting, and plot; some dialogue; events organized in chronological sequence with some flashbacks. In what genre has the student written?**

    A. Expository writing

    B. Narrative writing

    C. Persuasive writing

    D. Descriptive writing

Answer: B. Narrative writing

These are all characteristics of narrative writing. Expository writing is intended to give information such as an explanation or directions, and the information is logically organized. Persuasive writing gives an opinion in an attempt to convince the reader that this point of view is valid or tries to persuade the reader to take a specific action. The goal of technical writing is to clearly communicate a select piece of information to a targeted reader or group of readers for a particular purpose in such a way that the subject can readily be understood. It is persuasive writing that anticipates a response from the reader.

(Easy) (Skill 10.1)

23. **The main idea of a paragraph or story:**

    A. Is what the paragraph or story is about

    B. Indicates what the passage is about

    C. Gives more information about the topic

    D. States the important ideas that the author wants the reader to know about a topic

    Answer: D. States the important ideas that the author wants the reader to know about a topic.

    The main idea of a paragraph or story states the important ideas that the author wants the reader to know about his/her topic. The main idea can be directly stated or simply implied. The topic is what the paragraph or story is about. A topic sentence will indicate what a specific passage is about. And supporting details will give more information about a topic.

(Rigorous) (Skill 10.2)

24. **A strong topic sentence will:**

    A. Be phrased as a question.

    B. Always be the first sentence in a paragraph.

    C. Both A and B

    D. Neither A nor B

    Answer: D. Neither A nor B

    A topic sentence will tell what the passage is about. A tip for finding a topic sentence is to phrase the possible topic sentence as a question and see if the other sentences answer the question, but the topic sentence doesn't need to be in question form. A topic sentence is usually the first sentence in a paragraph but could also be in any other position. Therefore neither choices A nor B are correct choices.

(Average) (Skill 10.6)

25. **Which of the following is a great way to keep a natural atmosphere when speaking publicly?**

    A. Speak slowly

    B. Maintain a straight, but not stiff, posture

    C. Use friendly gestures

    D. Take a step to the side every once in a while

    Answer: C. Use friendly gestures.

    Gestures are a great way to keep a natural atmosphere when speaking publicly. Gestures that are common in friendly conversation will make the audience feel at ease. Gestures that are exaggerated, stiff, or awkward will only distract from a speech. Speaking slowly, monitoring posture, and taking a step to the side are great speaking skills but not skills that will create a natural atmosphere.

(Rigorous) (Skill 11.9)

26. **Students returning from a field trip to the local newspaper want to thank their hosts for the guided tour. As their teacher, what form of communication should you encourage them to use?**

    A. Each student will send an e-mail expressing his or her appreciation

    B. As a class, students will create a blog, and each student will write about what they learned

    C. Each student will write a thank you letter that the teacher will fax to the newspaper

    D. Each student will write a thank you note that the teacher will mail to the newspaper.

Answer: D. Each student will write a thank you note that the teacher will mail to the newspaper

Courtesy requires a hand-written message that is brief and specific. While using technology such as e-mails, blogs, and faxes are quicker, they are less personal. Communication channels and language styles vary; teachers should model correct behavior and appropriate uses of communication.

(Rigorous) (Skill 7.8)

27. **Which of the following skills can help students improve their listening comprehension?**

    I. Tap into prior knowledge.

    II. Look for transitions between ideas.

    III. Ask questions of the speaker.

    IV. Discuss the topic being presented.

    A. I and II only

    B. II and IV only

    C. II and IV only

    D. IV only

Answer: A. I and II only

Many strategies that are effective in improving reading comprehension are also effective in improving listening comprehension. Tapping into prior knowledge and looking for transitions between ideas are excellent listening and reading comprehension strategies. Asking questions of the speaker may help clarify ideas and discussing the topic may help organize the thoughts being presented, but both are difficult to do during the actual act of listening.

(Rigorous) (Skill 7.2)

28. **As Ms. Wolmark looks at the mandated vocabulary curriculum for the 3rd grade, she notes that she can opt to teach foreign words and abbreviations which have become part of the English language. She decides:**

    A. To forego that since she is not a teacher of foreign language

    B. To teach only foreign words from the native language of her four ELL students

    C. To use the ELL students' native languages as a start for an extensive study of foreign language words

    D. To teach 2-3 foreign language words that are now in English and let it go at that

Answer: C. To use the ELL students' native languages as a start for an extensive study of foreign language words

Incorporating the native language of ELL students into instruction helps to form a bond between their native language and English. It also serves as a point of confidence that connects that student with the other students in the class.

(Rigorous) (Skill 12.12)

29. Which of the following are good choices for supporting a thesis?

    A. Reasons
    B. Examples
    C. Answer to the question, "why?"
    D. All of the above

    Answer: D. All of the above

    The correct answer is D. When answering the question "why?" you are giving reasons, but those reasons need to be supported with examples.

Math

(Rigorous) (Skill 13.9)

30. A truck rental company charges $40 per day plus $2.50 per mile. The odometer reading is M miles when a customer rents a truck and m miles when it is returned d days later. Which expression represents the total charge for the rental?

    A. $40d + 2.5M - m$
    B. $40d + 2.5m - M$
    C. $40d + 2.5(M - m)$
    D. $40d + 2.5(m - M)$

    Answer: D. $40d + 2.5(m - M)$

Rental for d days is $40d$. The number of miles driven is $m - M$. The charge for miles driven is $2.50(m - M)$. Beginning mileage must be subtracted from ending mileage and the difference multiplied by 2.5.

(Easy) (Skill 13.1)

31. Using a pattern is an appropriate strategy for which of the following:

    I. Skip counting
    II. Counting backward
    III. Finding doubles

    A. I and II
    B. I and III
    C. II and III
    D. I, II, and III

    Answer: A. I and II

    The skip-counting pattern adds the same number repeatedly. Counting backward subtracts 1 repeatedly.

(Rigorous) (Skill 14.5)

32. The following set of numbers is not closed under addition:

    A. Set of all real numbers
    B. Set of all even numbers
    C. Set of all odd numbers
    D. Set of all rational numbers

    Answer: C. Set of all odd numbers

    Adding two real numbers will result in a real number. The same is true for even or rational numbers. Adding two odd numbers, however, will not always produce an odd number.

(Rigorous) (Skill 14.3)

33. What is the value of the following expression?

$$\frac{5 - 2(6 - 2 \cdot 3)}{-5(2 + 2 \cdot 4)}$$

A. 0.5

B. 5.0

C. -0.5

D. 3.4

Answer: C. -0.5

The fraction line is equivalent to parentheses and indicates that the numerator is to be simplified first. Then use the standard order of operations.

(Average) (Skill 14.4)

34. Which of the following expressions are equivalent to $28 - 4 \cdot 6 + 12$?

I. $(28 - 4) \cdot 6 + 12$
II. $28 - (4 \cdot 6) + 12$
III. $(28 - 4) \cdot (6 + 12)$
IV. $(28 + 12) - (4 \cdot 6)$
V. $28 - 4 \cdot 12 + 6$

A. I and V

B. II and IV

C. III and V

D. IV and V

Answer: B. II and IV

The parentheses in expression II indicate that the multiplication is to be done first. Using the standard order of operations: multiply and divide from left to right, then add and subtract from left to right.

(Average) (Skill 15.1)

35. If n represents an odd number, which of the following does not represent an even number?

A. $2n$

B. $2(n + 1)$

C. n^2

D. $10n - 2$

Answer: C. n^2

n^2 represents an odd number times an odd number, which will be an odd number. Choices A, B, and D are multiples of 2 and represent even numbers.

(Rigorous) (Skill 15.5)

36. Based upon the following examples, can you conclude that the sum of two prime numbers is also a prime number? Why or why not?

$2 + 3 = 5$

$2 + 5 = 7$

$11 + 2 = 13$

A. Yes; there is a pattern

B. Yes; there are many more examples, such as $17 + 2 = 19$ and $29 + 2 = 31$

C. No; there are many counterexamples

D. No; the sums are not prime numbers

Answer: C. No; there are many counterexamples

Only one counterexample is needed to disprove a statement. For example, in $3 + 5 = 8$ the sum is a composite number.

Care must be taken not to generalize a perceived pattern based upon too few examples. Additional examples are not sufficient to establish a pattern. In choice D, 5, 7, and 13 are prime numbers.

(Rigorous) (Skill 15.6)

37. If x is a whole number, what is the best description of the number $4x + 1$?

    A. Prime number
    B. Composite number
    C. Odd number
    D. Even number

Answer: C. Odd number

Since $4x$ is a multiple of 4, it is an even number. One more than an even number is an odd number. The prime numbers do not follow a pattern. $4x + 1$ may be either prime, for example 13, or composite, for example 9.

(Rigorous) (Skill 15.8)

38. The plot for a proposed new city hall plaza is 120 feet long by 90 feet wide. A scale model for the plaza must fit in an area that is 10 feet square. If the largest possible model is built in that area, what will be the maximum possible width for the scale model?

    A. $\frac{2}{15}$ ft
    B. $1\frac{1}{3}$ ft
    C. $7\frac{1}{2}$ ft
    D. $13\frac{1}{3}$ ft

Answer: C. $7\frac{1}{2}$ ft

Use a proportion to find the maximum width:

$$\frac{120}{10} = \frac{90}{x} \rightarrow x = 7\frac{1}{2}$$

The maximum width is $7\frac{1}{2}$ ft. Be sure to set up the proportion with equivalent ratios to find the maximum width. Check for reasonableness of results. The width cannot exceed 10 ft.

(Easy) (Skill 17.2)

39. Jocelyn wants create a magnetic board in the back of her classroom by covering part of the wall with a special magnetic paint. Each can of paint will cover 15 square feet. If the area is 12 feet wide and 8 feet high, how many cans of paint should she buy?

    A. 5 cans
    B. 6 cans
    C. 7 cans
    D. 8 cans

Answer: C. 7 cans

First, find the area of the magnetic board. Then divide by 15.

$12 \times 8 = 96$
$96 \div 15 = 6.4$

Jocelyn cannot buy 6.4 cans. She must buy 7 cans. Consider the meaning of any remainder in the context of the problem.

(Easy) (Skill 15.3)

40. A recipe makes 6 servings and calls for $1\frac{1}{2}$ cups of rice. How much rice is needed to make 10 servings?

   A. 2 cups
   B. $2\frac{1}{4}$ cups
   C. $2\frac{1}{2}$ cups
   D. $2\frac{3}{4}$ cups

Answer: C. $2\frac{1}{2}$ cups

Write and solve a proportion.

$\frac{1.5}{6} = \frac{x}{10}$

$1.5(10) = 6x$

$x = 2.5$

When writing a proportion, check that the ratios are equivalent:

$\frac{\text{cups of rice}}{\text{servings}} = \frac{\text{cups of rice}}{\text{servings}}$

(Rigorous) (Skill 15.10)

41. Which table(s) represents solutions of the following equation?

I.
x	-5	0	5	10
y	-12	-10	-8	-6

II.
x	-5	0	5	-10
y	-12	-10	-12	-10

III.
x	20	25	30	35
y	-2	0	2	4

   A. I
   B. II
   C. II and III
   D. I and III

Answer: D. I and III

Substitute values for x and y into the equation. For example, if $x = -5$ and $y = -12$, then

$2(-5) - 5(-12) = 50$
$-10 - (-60) = 50$
$-10 + 60 = 50$

Since the equation is true, the values $x = -5$ and $y = -12$ are solutions of the equation.

In table II, substituting the values $x = 5$ and $y = -12$, gives a false statement since

$2(5) - 5(-12) = 50$
$10 - (-60) = 50$
$10 + 60 = 50$

(Average) (Skill 18.7)

42. The relations given below demonstrate the following addition and multiplication property of real numbers:

$a + b = b + a$

$ab = ba$

   A. Commutative
   B. Associative
   C. Identity
   D. Inverse

Answer: A. Commutative

Both addition and multiplication of real numbers satisfy the commutative property, according to which changing the order of the operands does not change the result of the operation.

(Rigorous) (Skill 15.4)

43. Which property (or properties) is applied below?

    $-8x + 5x = (-8 + 5)x$
    $= -3x$

    I. Associative Property of Addition
    II. Zero Property of Addition
    III. Additive Inverses
    IV. Identity Property of Multiplication
    V. Distributive Property

    A. I
    B. V
    C. I and III
    D. II and IV

    Answer: B. V

    The variable x is distributed over the sum of -8 and 5. Check definitions of properties.

(Rigorous) (Skill 15.2)

44. For which of the following is the additive inverse equal to the multiplicative inverse?

    A. $\frac{2}{3} + \frac{3}{2}$
    B. $\sqrt{-1}$
    C. $\frac{1 - \sqrt{2}}{1 + \sqrt{2}}$
    D. $(a + b) \div (b - a)$

    Answer: B. $\sqrt{-1}$

    Let the number for which the additive inverse is equal to the multiplicative inverse be x. Then $-x = \frac{1}{x}; \Rightarrow x^2 = -1; x = \sqrt{-1}$

(Rigorous) (Skill 14.2)

45. Which of the statements below explain the error(s), if any, in the following calculation?

    $\frac{18}{18} + 23 = 23$

    I. A number divided by itself is 1, not 0.
    II. The sum of 1 and 23 is 24, not 23.
    III. The 18s are "cancelled" and replaced by 0.

    A. I and II
    B. II and III
    C. I, II, and III
    D. There is no error.

    Answer: C. I, II, and III

    $\frac{18}{18}$ and $1 + 23 = 24$

(Average) (Skill 14.7)

46. Which statement is a model for the following problem?

    27 less than 5 times a number is 193.

    A. $27 < 5x + 193$
    B. $27 - 5x < 193$
    C. $5x - 27 < 193$
    D. $5x - 27 = 193$

    Answer: D. $5x - 27 = 193$

    5 times a number is represented by $5x$; 27 less than $5x$ by $5x - 27$; the difference *is* (equals) 193, not *is less than* 193. Avoid confusing *is less than* with *less than*.

(Average) (Skill 14.7)

47. What is the solution set of the following inequality?

$$4x + 9 \geq 11(x - 3)$$

A. $x \leq 0$

B. $x \geq 0$

C. $x \leq 6$

D. $x \geq 6$

Answer: C. $x \leq 6$

Apply the distributive property on the right.

$4x + 9 \geq 11(x - 3)$
$4x + 9 \geq 11x - 33$
$11x - 4x \leq 9 + 33$
$7x \leq 42$
$x \leq 6$

(Average) (Skill 13.2)

48. A car is rented in Quebec. The outside temperature shown on the dashboard reads 17°C. What is the temperature in degrees Fahrenheit? (Use the formula $F = \frac{9}{5}C + 32$.)

A. 27.2°F

B. 41.4°F

C. 62.6°F

D. 88.2°F

Answer: C. 62.6°F

Use the order of operations. First multiply $\frac{9}{5}$ and 17. Then add 32 to the result.

$F = (\frac{9}{5} + 17) + 32$
$= 30.6 + 32$
$= 62.6$

(Rigorous) (Skill 15.9)

49. The two solutions of the quadratic equation $ax^2 + bx + c = 0$ are given by the formula

$$x = \frac{-b \pm \sqrt{b^2 - 4ac}}{2a}.$$

What are the solutions of the equation $x^2 - 18x + 32$?

A. -5 and 23

B. 2 and 16

C. $9 \pm \sqrt{113}$

D. $9 \pm 2\sqrt{113}$

Answer: B. 2 and 16

Substitute in the formula: $a = 1$, $b = -18$, $c = 32$:

$$x = \frac{18 \pm \sqrt{18^2 - -4(32)}}{2}.$$

Then apply the standard order of operations: $x = \frac{18 + 14}{2}$ and $x = \frac{18 - 14}{2}$, or $x = 16$ and $x = 2$. Be sure to apply the standard order of operations after substituting in the formula.

(Rigorous) (Skill 16.2)

50. Triangle *ABC* is rotated 90° clockwise about the origin and translated 6 units left.

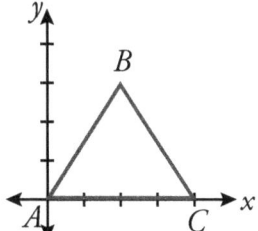

What are the coordinates of *B* after the transformations?

A. (2, –3)

B. (3, –2)

C. (–2, –3)

D. (–3, –2)

Answer: D. (–3, –2)

Under the rotation, (2, 3) → (3, -2). Sliding 6 units left, (3, -2) → (-3, -2). Work with one transformation at a time, rather than trying to do both at the same time.

(Easy) (Skill 16.1)

51. The following represents the net of a

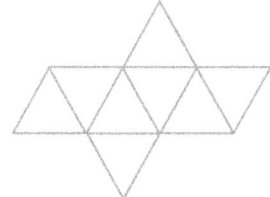

A. Cube

B. Tetrahedron

C. Octahedron

D. Dodecahedron

Answer: C. Octahedron

The eight equilateral triangles make up the eight faces of an octahedron.

(Rigorous) (Skill 16.4)

52. Ginny and Nick head back to their respective colleges after being home for the weekend. They leave their house at the same time and drive for 4 hours. Ginny drives due south at the average rate of 60 miles per hour and Nick drives due east at the average rate of 60 miles per hour. What is the straight-line distance between them, in miles, at the end of the 4 hours?

A. 169.7 miles

B. 240 miles

C. 288 miles

D. 339.4 miles

Answer: D. 339.4 miles

Ginny and Nick each drive a distance of 4 × 60, or 240 miles. Draw a diagram.

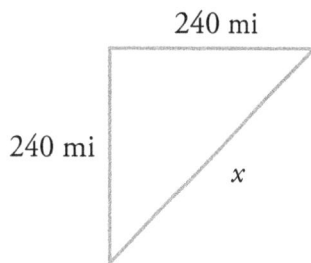

Then apply the Pythagorean Theorem:
$c^2 = a^2 + b^2$.
$x^2 = 240^2 + 240^2$
$= 115{,}200$
$x = \sqrt{115{,}200}$
$x \approx 339.4$

So *x* is about 339.4 miles. Be sure to use the standard order of operations when solving for *x*.

(Rigorous) (Skill 16.3)

53. **What is the surface area of the prism shown below?**

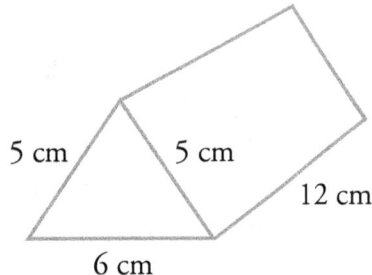

A. 204 cm²

B. 216 cm²

C. 360 cm²

D. 180 cm²

Answer: B. 216 cm²

Find the area of each face. Each triangular face has an altitude of 4 cm and area of 12 cm². Surface area = 5(12) + 5(12) + 6(12) + 12 + 12, which equals 216. Check that the areas of all the faces are included in the sum, especially the bottom and the back of the prism.

(Rigorous) (Skill 16.6)

54. **Find the area of a rectangle if you know that the base is 8 cm and the diagonal of the rectangle is 8.5 cm:**

A. 24 cm²

B. 30 cm²

C. 18.9 cm²

D. 24 cm

Answer: A. 24 cm²

The answer is A because the base of the rectangle is also one leg of the right triangle, and the diagonal is the hypotenuse of the triangle. To find the other leg of the triangle, you can use the Pythagorean theorem. Once you get the other leg of the triangle, that is also the height of the rectangle. To get the area, you multiply the base by the height. The reason the answer is A and not D is because area is measured in centimeters squared, not just centimeters.

(Average) (Skill 16.11)

55. **Which of the following is not equivalent to 3 km?**

I. 3.0×10^3 m

II. 3.0×10^4 cm

III. 3.0×10^6 mm

A. I

B. II

C. III

D. None of the above

Answer: B. II

There are 1000, or 10^3 meters in each kilometer; 100, or 10^2 cm, in each meter; and 10 millimeters in each centimeter. Remember to add exponents when multiplying: for example, 3.0×10^3 m = $3.0 \times 10^3 \times 10^2$ cm, or 3.0×10^5 cm.

(Average) (Skill 18.9)

56. **A school band has 200 members. Looking at the pie chart below, determine which statement is true about the band.**

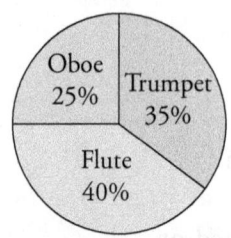

A. There are more trumpet players than flute players

B. There are fifty oboe players in the band

C. There are forty flute players in the band

D. One-third of all band members play the trumpet

Answer: B. There are fifty oboe players in the band

There are fifty oboe players in the band since 25% of 200 is 50.

(Rigorous) (Skill 18.5)

57. A restaurant offers the following menu choices.

Green Vegetable	Yellow Vegetable
Asparagus	Carrots
Broccoli	Corn
Peas	Squash
Spinach	

If a customer chooses a green vegetable and a yellow vegetable at random, what is the probability that the customer will order neither asparagus nor corn?

A. $\frac{1}{12}$

B. $\frac{1}{6}$

C. $\frac{1}{3}$

D. $\frac{1}{2}$

Answer: D. $\frac{1}{2}$

There are 4×3, or 12 possible combinations of choices. Of those, 6 include either asparagus or corn or both (1 asparagus and corn, 2 asparagus and not corn, and 3 corn but not asparagus). Since 6 out of the 12 choices are favorable, the probability is $\frac{6}{12}$, or $\frac{1}{2}$. Be careful not to count any choice (asparagus and corn) more than once.

(Rigorous) (Skill 17.4)

58. Given a drawer with 5 black socks, 3 blue socks, and 2 red socks, what is the probability that you will draw two black socks in two draws in a dark room?

A. $\frac{2}{9}$

B. $\frac{1}{4}$

C. $\frac{17}{18}$

D. $\frac{1}{18}$

Answer: A. $\frac{2}{9}$

In this example of conditional probability, the probability of drawing a black sock on the first draw is $\frac{5}{10}$. It is implied in the problem that there is no replacement, therefore the probability of obtaining a black sock in the second draw is $\frac{4}{9}$. Multiply the two probabilities and reduce to lowest terms.

(Rigorous) (Skill 18.3)

59. Find the inverse of the following statement: If I like dogs, then I do not like cats.

A. If I like dogs, then I do like cats.

B. If I like cats, then I like dogs.

C. If I like cats, then I do not like dogs.

D. If I do not like dogs, then I like cats.

Answer: D. If I do not like dogs, then I like cats.

When you take the inverse of the statement, you negate both statements. By negating both statements you take the opposite of the original statement.

(Average) (Skill 18.6)

60. A school has 15 male teachers and 35 female teachers. In how many ways can they form a committee with 2 male teachers and 4 female teachers on it?

    A. 525
    B. 5497800
    C. 88
    D. 263894400

Answer: B. 5497800

The number of ways one can pick 2 male teachers out of 15 =

$$^{15}_{2}C = \frac{15!}{13!2!} = \frac{14 \times 15}{2} = 105$$

The number of ways one can pick 4 female teachers out of 35 =

$$^{35}_{4}C = \frac{35!}{31!4!} = \frac{32 \times 33 \times 34 \times 35}{2 \times 3 \times 4} = 52360$$

Hence, the total number of ways the committee can be chosen = 105 × 52360 = 5497800.

(Rigorous) (Skill 18.8)

61. A music store owner wants to change the window display every week. Only 4 out of 6 instruments can be displayed in the window at the same time. How many weeks will it be before the owner must repeat the same arrangement (in the same order) of instruments in the window display?

    A. 24 weeks
    B. 36 weeks
    C. 120 weeks
    D. 360 weeks

Answer: D. 360 weeks

There are 6 choices for the first position. For each of those choices, there are 5 choices for the second position and 6 × 5 choices for the first two positions. For each of those there are 3 choices for the third position and 2 for the fourth position: 6 × 5 × 4 × 3 = 360.

(Rigorous) (Skill 18.2)

62. Half the students in a class scored 80% on an exam; one student scored 10%; and the rest of the class scored 85%. Which would be the best measure of central tendency for the test scores?

    A. Mean
    B. Median
    C. Mode
    D. Either the median or the mode because they are equal

Answer: B. Median

The median is the least sensitive to extreme values. The mode reports only one score and is not a reflection of the entire data set. The mean will be skewed by the outlier of 10%.

SOCIAL SCIENCES

(Average) (Skill 21.1)

63. The Great Plains in the United States are an excellent place to grow corn and wheat for all of the following reasons EXCEPT:

   A. Rainfall is abundant and the soil is rich
   B. The land is mostly flat and easy to cultivate
   C. The human population is modest in size, so there is plenty of space for large farms
   D. The climate is semitropical

   Answer: D. The climate is semitropical

   The climate on the Great Plains is not semitropical. It is temperate, with harsh winters. Rainfall and soil conditions are good. The land is flat. The human population is not overcrowded; there is room for large farms.

(Easy) (Skill 19.11)

64. Ms. Gomez has a number of ESOL students in her class. In order to meet their specific needs as second-language learners, which of the following would NOT be an appropriate approach?

   A. Pair students of different ability levels for English practice
   B. Focus most of her instruction on teaching English rather than content
   C. Provide accommodations during testing and with assignments
   D. Use visual aids to help students make word links with familiar objects

   Answer: B. Focus most of her instruction on teaching English rather than content

   In working with ESOL students, different approaches should be used to ensure that students (a) Get multiple opportunities to learn and practice English, and (b) Still learn content. Content should not be given short shrift or be "dumbed down" for ESOL students.

(Average) (Skill 22.8)

65. In the 1800s, the era of industrialization and growth was characterized by:

   A. Small firms
   B. Public ownership
   C. Worker-owned enterprises
   D. Monopolies and trusts

   Answer: D. Monopolies and trusts

   The era of industrialization and business expansion was characterized by big businesses and monopolies that merged into trusts. There were few small firms and there was no public ownership or worker-owned enterprises.

(Rigorous) (Skill 21.22)

66. What is characteristic of areas of the world with high populations?

   A. These areas tend to have heavy pollution
   B. These areas are almost always surrounded by suburbs
   C. Populations are rarely located near one another
   D. Most populated places in the world also tend to be close to agricultural lands

Answer: D. Most populated places in the world also tend to be close to agricultural lands.

Pollution (choice A) and suburbs (choice B) are often found in populated areas, but they are not always present and are not mentioned in the text. The text says that population centers are often, not rarely (choice C), located near each other.

(Average) (Skill 22.8)
67. In the 1800s, the era of industrialization and growth was characterized by:
   A. Small firms
   B. Public ownership
   C. Worker-owned enterprises
   D. Monopolies and trusts

Answer: D. Monopolies and trusts

The era of industrialization and business expansion was characterized by big businesses and monopolies that merged into trusts. There were few small firms and there was no public ownership or worker-owned enterprises.

(Average) (Skill 21.20)
68. Meridians, or lines of longitude, not only help in pinpointing locations but are also used for:
   A. Measuring distance from the Poles
   B. Determining direction of ocean currents
   C. Determining the time around the world
   D. Measuring distance on the equator

Answer: C. Determining the time around the world

Meridians, or lines of longitude, are the determining factor in separating time zones and determining time around the world.

(Rigorous) (Skill 21.16)
69. The Western Hemisphere contains all of which of the following continents?
   A. Russia
   B. Europe
   C. North America
   D. Asia

Answer: C North America

The Western Hemisphere, located between the North and South Poles and between the Prime Meridian (0 degrees longitude) west to the International Date Line at 180 degrees longitude, consists of all of North and South America, a tiny part of the easternmost part of Russia that extends east of 180 degrees longitude, and a part of Europe that extends west of the Prime Meridian (0 degrees longitude).

(Rigorous) (Skill 21.19)
70. Mr. Allen is discussing the earthquake in Chile and explains the aftershocks and tsunamis that threatened Pacific islands thousands of miles away. What aspect of geographical studies was he emphasizing?
   A. Regional
   B. Topical
   C. Physical
   D. Human

Answer: C. Physical

Earthquakes, aftershocks, and tsunamis are physical features on the earth. Regional studies would focus on the elements or characteristics of a particular region, such as in Chile itself. Topical studies focus on an earth feature or human activity occurring throughout the entire world, such as talking about earthquakes in Italy, Haiti, Chile, Mexico and other countries. Human studies would focus on human activity patterns and how they relate to the environment including political, cultural, historical, urban, and social geographical fields of study.

(Average) (Skill 21.11)

71. Which of the following are non-renewable resources?

    A. Fish, coffee, and forests
    B. Fruit, water, and solar energy
    C. Wind power, alcohol, and sugar
    D. Coal, natural gas, and oil

Answer: D. Coal, natural gas, and oil

Coal, natural gas, and oil are fossil fuels, which cannot be renewed. Nonrenewable resources are natural resources that cannot be remade or regenerated in the same proportion that they are used. Renewable resources are generally living resources (fish, coffee, and forests, for example), which can restock (renew) themselves if they are not over harvested. Renewable resources can restock themselves and be used indefinitely if they are sustained.

(Average) (Skill 21.23)

72. What people perfected the preservation of dead bodies?

    A. Sumerians
    B. Phoenicians
    C. Egyptians
    D. Assyrians

Answer: C. Egyptians

The Sumerians (choice A), Phoenicians (choice B), and Assyrians (choice D) all made contributions to ancient civilization but preserving dead bodies was not among their respective contributions.

(Rigorous) (Skill 21.9)

73. Which of these is NOT a true statement about the Roman civilization?

    A. Its period of Pax Romana provided long periods of peace during which travel and trade increased, enabling the spread of culture, goods, and ideas over the known world
    B. It borrowed the concept of democracy from the Greeks and developed it into a complex representative government
    C. It flourished in the arts with a realistic approach to art and a dramatic use of architecture
    D. It developed agricultural innovations such as crop rotation and terrace farming

Answer: D. It developed agricultural innovations such as crop rotation and terrace farming

China developed crop rotation and terrace farming.

(Average) (Skill 23.6)

74. The major force in eighteenth and nineteenth century politics was:

    A. Nationalism
    B. Revolution
    C. War
    D. Diplomacy

Answer: A. Nationalism

Nationalism was the driving force in politics in the eighteenth and nineteenth century. Groups of people that shared common traits and characteristics wanted their own government and countries. This led to some revolution, war, and the failure of diplomacy.

(Average) (Skill 21.14)

75. The identification of individuals or groups as they are influenced by their own group or culture is called:

    A. Cross-cultural exchanges
    B. Cultural diffusion
    C. Cultural identity
    D. Cosmopolitanism

Answer: C. Cultural identity

Cross-cultural exchanges involved the discovery of shared values and needs as well as an appreciation of differences. Cultural diffusion is the movement of cultural ideas or materials between populations independent of the movement of those populations. Cosmopolitanism blurs cultural differences in the creation of a shared new culture.

(Average) (Skill 20.24)

76. The New England colonies included:

    A. South Carolina
    B. Georgia
    C. Massachusetts
    D. New York

Answer: C. Massachusetts

South Carolina (choice A) and Georgia (choice B) were southern colonies. New York (choice D) was a middle Atlantic colony.

(Rigorous) (Skill 20.22)

77. Which major economic activity of the Southern colonies led to the growth of slavery?

    A. Manufacturing
    B. Fishing
    C. Farming
    D. Coal mining

Answer: C. Farming

The major economic activity in this region was farming. Here the soil was very fertile, and the climate was very mild with an even longer growing season than farther north. The large plantations, eventually requiring large numbers of slaves, were found in the coastal or tidewater areas. Although the wealthy slave-owning planters set the pattern of life in this region, most of the people lived inland away from coastal areas. They were small farmers and very few, if any, owned slaves.

(Average) (Skill 20.18)

78. **Which was the first instance of an internal tax on the American colonies?**

    A. The Proclamation Act

    B. The Sugar Act

    C. The Currency Act

    D. The Stamp Act

Answer: D. The Stamp Act

The Proclamation Act prohibited English settlement beyond the Appalachian Mountains to appease the Native Americans. The Sugar Act imposed a tax on foreign molasses, sugar, and other goods imported into the colonies. The Currency Act prohibited colonial governments from issuing paper money. The Stamp Act placed a tax on newspapers, legal documents, licenses, almanacs, and playing cards which made it the first instance of an "internal" tax on the colonies.

(Average) (Skill 20.19)

79. **The Lewis and Clark expedition advanced knowledge in each of the following areas EXCEPT:**

    A. Geography

    B. Modern warfare

    C. Botany

    D. Animal life

Answer: B. Modern warfare

The Lewis and Clark expedition was peaceful. Lewis and Clark learned a great deal about geography, botany, and animal life.

(Average) (Skill 20.23)

80. **Populism arises out of a feeling:**

    A. Of intense happiness

    B. Of satisfaction with the activities of large corporations

    C. That women should not be allowed to vote

    D. Perceived oppression

Answer: D. Perceived oppression

Perceived oppression felt by average people toward the wealthy elite gave rise to Populism. Populists do not become prominent when people are happy (choice A), or when people are satisfied with the activities of large corporations (choice B). Populists and other progressives fought for, not against (choice C), voting rights for women.

(Average) (Skill 20.16)

81. **At the end of the Twentieth Century, the United States was:**

    A. A central leader in international affairs

    B. A reluctant participant in international affairs

    C. One of two superpowers

    D. Lacking a large consumer culture

Answer: A. A central leader in international affairs

It was a reluctant participant (choice B) in international affairs at the beginning of the twentieth century. The United States was the only superpower (choice C) left at the end of the twentieth century. The United States developed a large consumer culture (choice D) in the 1950s and still has it today.

(Rigorous) (Skill 20.17)

82. How did manufacturing change in the early 1800s?

   A. The electronics industry was born
   B. Production moved from small shops or homes into factories
   C. Industry benefited from the Federal Reserve Act
   D. The timber industry was hurt when Theodore Roosevelt set aside 238 million acres of federal lands to be protected from development

Answer: B. Production moved from small shops or homes into factories

Factories had modern machinery in them that could produce goods efficiently. The electronics industry (choice A) did not exist in the early 1800s. The Federal Reserve Act (choice C) came much later, in the Twentieth Century. Theodore Roosevelt's protection of federal lands from development (choice D) also took place in the Twentieth Century.

(Rigorous) (Skill 22.7)

83. The early ancient civilizations developed systems of government:

   A. To provide for defense against attack
   B. To regulate trade
   C. To regulate and direct the economic activities of the people as they worked together in groups
   D. To decide on the boundaries of the different fields during planting seasons

Answer: C. To regulate and direct the economic activities of the people as they worked together in groups

Although ancient civilizations were concerned with defense, trade regulation, and the maintenance of boundaries in their fields, they could not have done any of them without first regulating and directing the economic activities of the people as they worked in groups. This provided for a stable economic base from which they could trade and actually had something worth providing defense for.

(Rigorous) (Skill 20.1)

84. What is another name for dictatorship?

   A. Oligarchy
   B. Monarchy
   C. Anarchism
   D. Communism

Answer: A. Oligarchy

Monarchy (choice B) features a king or a queen, not a dictator. Anarchism (choice C) favors the elimination of all government and its replacement by a cooperative community of individuals. Dictatorship is not about cooperating between individuals. Communism (choice D) is decentralized, while dictatorship is highly centralized.

(Average) (Skill 23.3)

85. Which of the following documents described and defined the system and structure of the United States government?

   A. The Bill of Rights
   B. The Declaration of Independence
   C. The Constitution
   D. The Articles of Confederation

Answer: C. The Constitution

The United States Constitution is the written document that describes and defines the system and structure of the United States government. The first ten Amendments to the Constitution are called the Bill of Rights. The Declaration of Independence, written in 1776 by Thomas Jefferson, was a call to the colonies to unite against the King, detailing the grievances of the colonies and articulating the philosophical framework upon which the United States is founded. The Articles of Confederation were the first attempt of the newly independent states to reach a new understanding among themselves.

(Rigorous) (Skill 23.4)

86. How did the ideology of John Locke influence Thomas Jefferson in writing the Declaration of Independence?

    A. Locke emphasized human rights and believed that people should rebel against governments who violated those rights
    B. Locke emphasized the rights of government to protect its people and to levy taxes
    C. Locke believed in the British system of monarchy and the rights of Parliament to make laws
    D. Locke advocated individual rights over the collective whole

Answer: A. Locke emphasized human rights and believed that people should rebel against governments who violated those rights

The Declaration of Independence is an outgrowth of both ancient Greek ideas of democracy and individual rights and the ideas of the European Enlightenment and the Renaissance, especially the ideology of the political thinker John Locke. Thomas Jefferson (1743–1826) the principle author of the Declaration borrowed much from Locke's theories and writings. John Locke was one of the most influential political writers of the seventeenth century who put great emphasis on human rights and put forth the belief that when governments violate those rights people should rebel. He wrote the book *Two Treatises of Government* in 1690, which had tremendous influence on political thought in the American colonies and helped shape the U.S. Constitution and Declaration of Independence.

(Average) (Skill 23.1)

87. Which of the following is not a right declared by the U.S. Constitution?

    A. The right to speak out in public
    B. The right to use cruel and unusual punishment
    C. The right to a speedy trial
    D. The right not to be forced to testify against yourself

Answer: B The right to use cruel and unusual punishment.

A person who lives in a democratic society legally has a comprehensive list of rights guaranteed to him or her by the government. In the United States, this is the Constitution and its Amendments. Among these very important rights are:

- the right to speak out in public;
- the right to pursue any religion;

- the right for a group of people to gather in public for any reason that doesn't fall under a national security cloud;
- the right not to have soldiers stationed in your home;
- the right not to be forced to testify against yourself in a court of law;
- the right to a speedy and public trial by a jury of your peers;
- the right not to be the victim of cruel and unusual punishment; and
- the right to avoid unreasonable search and seizure of your person, your house, and your vehicle.

(Rigorous) (Skill 22.5)

88. The cold weather froze orange crops in Florida and the price of orange juice increased. This is an example of what economic concept?

    A. Output market
    B. Input market
    C. Supply and demand
    D. Entrepreneurship

Answer: C. Supply and demand.

Output markets refer to the market in which goods and services are sold. The *input market* is the market in which factors of production, or resources, are bought and sold.

(Average) (Skill 22.4)

89. What type of production process must producers choose?

    A. One that is inefficient
    B. One that often produces goods that consumers don't want
    C. One that is efficient
    D. One that is sometimes efficient and sometimes inefficient

Answer: C. One that is efficient.

Producers cannot stay in business if they operate inefficiently (choice A). Producers cannot afford to produce goods that consumers don't want (choice B). Producers will suffer if their efficiency is inconsistent (choice D).

(Rigorous) (Skill 22.6)

90. The existence of economics is based on:

    A. The scarcity of resources
    B. The abundance of resources
    C. Little or nothing that is related to resources
    D. Entrepreneurship

Answer: A. The scarcity of resources.

If resources were always abundant (choice B), economics would be unnecessary. Economics is closely, not loosely (choice C) related to resources. Entrepreneurship (choice D) is part of economitcs, but is not the primary basis of economics.

(Rigorous) (Skill 22.2)

91. In the fictional country of Nacirema, the government controls the means of production and directs resources. It alone decides what will be produced; as a result, there is an abundance of capital and military goods but a scarcity of consumer goods. What type of economy is this?

    A. Market economy

    B. Centrally planned economy

    C. Market socialism

    D. Capitalism

Answer: B. Centrally planned economy.

In a planned economy, the means of production are publicly owned, with little, if any private ownership. Instead of the "three questions" being solved by markets, there is a planning authority that makes the decisions. The planning authority decides what will be produced and how. Since most planned economies direct resources into the production of capital and military goods, there is little remaining for consumer goods; the result is often chronic shortages.

(Average) (Skill 19.8)

92. Which of the following are secondary research materials?

    A. The conclusions and inferences of other historians

    B. Literature and nonverbal materials, novels, stories, poetry, and essays from the period, as well as coins, archaeological artifacts, and art produced during the period

    C. Interviews and surveys conducted by the researcher

    D. Statistics gathered as the result of the research's experiments

Answer: A. The conclusions and inferences of other historians

Secondary sources are works written significantly after the period being studied and based upon primary sources. In this case, historians have studied artifacts of the time and drawn their conclusion and inferences. Primary sources are the basic materials that provide raw data and information. Students or researchers may use literature and other data they have collected to draw their own conclusions or inferences.

(Rigorous) (Skill 19.6)

93. For their research paper on the effects of the Civil War on American literature, students have brainstormed a list of potential online sources and are seeking your authorization. Which of these represent the strongest source?

    A. http://www.wikipedia.org/

    B. http://www.google.com

    C. http://www.nytimes.com

    D. http://docsouth.unc.edu/southlit/civilwar.html

Answer: D. http://docsouth.unc.edu/southlit/civilwar.html

Sites with an "edu" domain are associated with educational institutions and tend to be more trustworthy for research information. Wikipedia has an "org" domain, which means it is a nonprofit. While Wikipedia may be appropriate for background reading, its credibility as a research site is questionable. Both Google and the New York Times are "com" sites, which are for profit. Even though this does not discredit their information, each site is problematic for researchers. With Google, students will get overwhelmed with hits and may not choose the most reputable sites for their information. As a newspaper, the New York Times would not be a strong source for historical information.

(Rigorous) (Skill 19.7)

94. **For the historian studying ancient Egypt, which of the following would be least useful?**

    A. The record of an ancient Greek historian on Greek-Egyptian interaction
    B. Letters from an Egyptian ruler to his/her regional governors
    C. Inscriptions on stele of the Fourteenth Egyptian Dynasty
    D. Letters from a nineteenth century Egyptologist to his wife

Answer: D. Letters from a nineteenth century Egyptologist to his wife

Historians use primary sources from the actual time they are studying whenever possible. Ancient Greek records of interaction with Egypt (choice A), letters from an Egyptian ruler to regional governors (choice B), and inscriptions from the Fourteenth Egyptian Dynasty (choice C) are all primary sources created at or near the actual time being studied. Choice D, letters from a nineteenth century Egyptologist, would not be considered primary sources, as they were created thousands of years after the fact and may not actually be about the subject being studied.

(Rigorous) (Skill 19.1)

95. **Which of the following can be considered the primary goal of social studies?**

    A. Recalling specific dates and places
    B. Identifying and analyzing social links
    C. Using contextual clues to identify eras
    D. Linking experiments with history

Answer: B. Identifying and analyzing social links

Historic events and social issues cannot be considered only in isolation. People and their actions are connected in many ways, and events are linked through cause and effect over time. Identifying and analyzing these social and historic links is a primary goal of the social sciences. The methods used to analyze social phenomena borrow from several of the social sciences. Interviews, statistical evaluation, observation, and experimentation are just some of the ways that people's opinions and motivations can be measured. From these opinions, larger social beliefs and movements can be interpreted, and events, issues and social problems can be placed in context to provide a fuller view of their importance.

SCIENCE

(Easy) (Skill 38.1)

96. Which is the correct order for the layers of Earth's atmosphere?

    A. Troposphere, stratosphere, mesosphere, and thermosphere
    B. Mesosphere, stratosphere, troposphere, and thermosphere
    C. Troposphere, stratosphere, thermosphere, and mesosphere
    D. Thermosphere, troposphere, stratosphere, mesosphere

Answer: A. Troposphere, stratosphere, mesosphere, and thermosphere

All weather occurs in the troposphere. There are few clouds in the stratosphere, but weather balloons can float in this region. Air temperatures start to drop in the mesosphere. The coldest spot on Earth is where the mesosphere meets the thermosphere. The thermosphere extends into outer space.

(Rigorous) (Skill 34.2)

97. What kind of chemical reaction is photosynthesis?

    A. Fusion
    B. Exothermic
    C. Endothermic
    D. Could be exothermic or endothermic

Answer: D. Could be exothermic or endothermic

Photosynthesis combines oxygen with carbon. When carbon burns heat is given off, so combining carbon and oxygen is exothermic. But with photosynthesis, radiant energy is used. Fusion refers to the combining of nuclei, not atoms.

(Easy) (Skill 39.1)

98. What type of rock can be classified by the size of the crystals in the rock?

    A. Metamorphic
    B. Igneous
    C. Minerals
    D. Sedimentary

Answer: B. Igneous

Igneous rock is formed when molten rock material cools. It is characterized by its grain size and mineral content. Metamorphic rocks are formed from other rocks as a result of heat and pressure. Sedimentary rocks come from weathering and erosion of pre existing rocks.

(Easy) (Skill 36.2)

99. In which of the following eras did life appear?

    A. Paleozoic
    B. Mesozoic
    C. Cenozoic
    D. Precambrian

Answer: D. Precambrian

The Cambrian explosion, the rapid appearance of most groups of complex organisms, took place in the Cambrian period, which is part of the Paleozoic era. Humans evolved in the Cenozoic era, dinosaurs in the Mesozoic era, and fish in the Paleozoic era.

(Easy) (Skill 39.5)

100. **The use of radioactivity to determine the age of rocks and fossils is called which of the following?**

    A. Carbon dating

    B. Absolute dating

    C. Stratigraphy

    D. Geological dating

    Answer: B. Absolute dating

    Carbon dating measures the relative amount of carbon-14, which is radioactive, with the amount of carbon-12. The ratio of carbon-12 and carbon-14 in an organic substance at different points in time is known. Stratigraphy is the study or rock layers.

(Easy) (Skill 41.1)

101. **Which of the following astronomical entities is not part of the galaxy the Sun is located in?**

    A. Nebulae

    B. Quasars

    C. Pulsars

    D. Neutron stars

    Answer: B. Quasars

    Nebulae are visible in the night sky and are glowing clouds of dust, hydrogen, and plasma. Neutron stars are the remnants of super novae, and pulsars are neutron stars that emit radio waves on a periodic basis. A quasar is a distant galaxy that emits large amounts of visible light and radio waves.

(Average) (Skill 41.2)

102. **Why is the winter in the southern hemisphere colder than winter in the northern hemisphere?**

    A. Earth's axis of 24-hour rotation tilts at an angle of $23\frac{1}{2}$

    B. The elliptical orbit of Earth around the Sun changes the distance of the Sun from Earth

    C. The southern hemisphere has more water than the northern hemisphere

    D. The green house effect is greater for the northern hemisphere

    Answer: B. The elliptical orbit of Earth around the Sun changes the distance of the Sun from Earth

    The tilt of Earth's axis causes the seasons. The Earth is close to the Sun during winter in the northern hemisphere. Winter in the southern hemisphere occurs six months later when Earth is farther from the Sun. The presence of water explains why winters are harsher inland than by the coast.

(Average) (Skill 34.1)

103. **Which of the following is not a property that eukaryotes have and prokaryotes do not have?**

    A. Nucleus

    B. Ribosomes

    C. Chromosomes

    D. Mitochondria

    Answer: B. Ribosomes

    Prokaryotes do not have a nuclear membrane, and the DNA is not packed into chromosomes. Mitochondria are organelles that produce power are not in the smaller, simpler cell. Ribosomes are the sites where cells assemble proteins.

(Easy) (Skill 34.4)

104. **Which of the following processes and packages macromolecules?**

    A. Lysosomes

    B. Cytosol

    C. Golgi apparatus

    D. Plastids

    Answer: C. Golgi apparatus

    Lysosomes contain digestive enzymes. Cytosol is the liquid inside cells. Plastids manufacture chemicals used in plant cells.

(Easy) (Skill 35.1)

105. **Which is not a characteristic of living organisms?**

    A. Sexual reproduction

    B. Ingestion

    C. Synthesis

    D. Respiration

    Answer: A. Sexual reproduction

    Only certain organisms reproduce sexually, that is by mixing DNA. Single-celled organisms generally reproduce by cell division. Ingestion means taking nutrients from outside the cell wall. Synthesis means creating new cellular material. Respiration means generating energy by combining oxygen or some other gas with material in the cell.

(Average) (Skill 35.3)

106. **At what stage in mitosis does the chromatin become chromosomes?**

    A. Telophase

    B. Anaphase

    C. Prophase

    D. Metaphase

    Answer: C. Prophase

    Prophase is the beginning of mitosis. In metaphase, fibers attach to chromosomes, and in anaphase, the chromosomes separate. In telophase, the cells divide.

(Average) (Skill 36.1)

107. **Which of the following is not part of Darwinian evolution?**

    A. Survival of the fittest

    B. Random mutations

    C. Heritability of acquired traits

    D. Natural selection

    Answer: C. Heritability of acquired traits

    Acquired traits change somatic cells but not gametes. So they are not passed on to succeeding generations. Natural selection occurs because offspring through random mutations are more fit than others to survive. The idea that acquired traits can be passed on to offspring is called Lamarkism.

(Easy) (Skill 37.3)

108. Taxonomy classifies species into genera (plural of genus) based on similarities. Species are subordinate to genera. The most general or highest taxonomical group is the kingdom. Which of the following is the correct order of the other groups from highest to lowest?

    A. Class ⇒ order ⇒ family ⇒ phylum
    B. Phylum ⇒ class ⇒ family ⇒ order
    C. Phylum ⇒ class ⇒ order ⇒ family
    D. Order ⇒ phylum ⇒ class ⇒ family

    Answer: C. Phylum ⇒ class ⇒ order ⇒ family

    In the case of the domestic dog, the genus (Canis) includes wolves, the family (Canidae) includes jackals and coyotes, the order (Carnivore) includes lions, the class (Mammals) includes mice, and the phylum (Chordata) includes fish.

(Easy) (Skill 36.3)

109. Which of the following describes the interaction between community members when one species feeds of another species but does not kill it immediately?

    A. Parasitism
    B. Predation
    C. Commensalism
    D. Mutualism

    Answer: A. Parasitism

    Predation occurs when one species kills another species. In mutualism, both species benefit. In commensalisms, one species benefits without the other being harmed.

(Easy) (Skill 31.3)

110. Which of the following statements about the density of a substance is true?

    A. It is a chemical property
    B. It is a physical property
    C. It does not depend on the temperature of the substance
    D. It is a property only of liquids and solids

    Answer: B. It is a physical property

    The density of a substance is the mass of an object made of the substance divided by the object's volume. Chemical properties involve chemical reactions. Densities of substances generally decrease with higher temperatures.

(Easy) (Skill 31.1)

111. The electrons in a neutral atom that is not in an excited energy state are in various energy shells. For example, there are two electrons in the lowest energy shell and eight in the next shell if the atom contains more than 10 electrons. How many electrons are in the shell with the maximum number of electrons?

    A. 8
    B. 18
    C. 32
    D. 44

    Answer: C. 32

    There is no energy level with 44 electrons. There is however, a shell with 18 electrons. The number of electrons in an atom's outer shell determines how the atom chemically interacts with other atoms.

(Rigorous) (Skill 27.1)

112. Which statement best explains why a balance scale is used to measure both weight and mass?

    A. The weight and mass of an object are identical concepts
    B. The force of gravity between two objects depends on the mass of the two objects
    C. Inertial mass and gravitational mass are identical
    D. A balance scale compares the weight of two objects

Answer: C. Inertial mass and gravitational mass are identical

The mass of an object is a fundamental property of matter and is measured in kilograms. The weight is the force of gravity between Earth and an object near Earth's surface and is measured in newtons or pounds. Newton's second law ($F = ma$) and the universal law of gravity ($F = G \frac{m_{earth} m}{d^2}$) determine the weight of an object. The mass in Newton's second law is called the inertial mass and the mass in the universal law of gravity is called the gravitational mass. The two kinds of masses are identical.

(Average) (Skill 30.3)

113. Which of the following does not determine the frictional force between a box sliding down a ramp?

    A. The weight of the box
    B. The area of the box
    C. The angle the ramp makes with the horizontal
    D. The chemical properties of the two surfaces

Answer: B. The area of the box

The frictional force is caused by bonding between the molecules of the box with the molecules of the ramp. At a small number of points, there is contact between the molecules. While there may be a small increase in the frictional force as the area increases, it is not noticeable. The main determinant of the frictional force is the weight of the box and the nature of the two surfaces.

(Easy) (Skill 40.1)

114. Which statement is true about temperature?

    A. Temperature is a measurement of heat
    B. Temperature is how hot or cold an object is
    C. The coldest temperature ever measured is zero degrees Kelvin
    D. The temperature of a molecule is its kinetic energy

Answer: B. Temperature is how hot or cold an object is

Temperature is a physical property of objects relating to how they feel when touched. For example, 0 degrees Celsius or 32 degrees Fahrenheit is defined as the temperature of ice water. Heat is a form of energy that flows from hot objects in thermal contact with cold objects. The greater the temperature of an object, the greater the kinetic energy of the molecules making up the object, but a single molecule does not have a temperature. The third law of thermodynamics is that absolute zero can never be achieved in a laboratory.

(Rigorous) (Skill 32.2)

115. When glass is heated, it becomes softer and softer until it becomes a liquid. Which of the following statements best describes this phenomenon?

   A. Glass has no heat of vaporization
   B. Glass has no heat of fusion
   C. The latent heat of glass is zero calories per gram
   D. Glass is made up of crystals

Answer: B. Glass has no heat of fusion

When a substance goes from the solid state to the liquid state as heat is added at the melting point, the temperature is constant. All the heat energy goes into changing the forces between the atoms, ions, or molecules so that the substance becomes a liquid. The heat of vaporization is the calories of heat needed to change one gram of the liquid into a gas.

(Average) (Skill 32.1)

116. Which statement could be described as the first law of thermodynamics?

   A. No machine can convert heat energy to work with 100 percent efficiency
   B. Energy is neither created nor destroyed
   C. Thermometers can be used to measure temperatures
   D. Heat flows from hot objects to cold objects

Answer: B. Energy is neither created nor destroyed

The first law of thermodynamics is considered to be a statement of the conservation of energy. Choices B and D are statements of the second law of thermodynamics. Answer C is the zeroth law of thermodynamics.

(Average) (Skill 31.6)

117. What kind of chemical reaction is the burning of coal?

   A. Exothermic and composition
   B. Exothermic and decomposition
   C. Endothermic and composition
   D. Endothermic and decomposition

Answer: A. Exothermic and composition

Burning coal means oxygen is combining with carbon to produce carbon dioxide. Since heat is released, the reaction is exothermic. Since elements are combining to for a compound, the reaction is a composition.

(Easy) (Skill 33.3)

118. Which of the following is a result of a nuclear reaction called fission?

   A. Sunlight
   B. Cosmic radiation
   C. Supernova
   D. Existence of the elements in the periodic table

Answer: D. Existence of the elements in the periodic table

Sunlight comes from fusion. Cosmic radiation has many sources. Inside stars, hydrogen and helium combine to form the higher elements on the periodic table.

(Easy) (Skill 25.3)

119. What is technology?

    A. The application of science to satisfy human needs

    B. Knowledge of complex machines, computer systems, and manufacturing processes

    C. The study of engineering

    D. A branch of science

    Answer: A. The application of science to satisfy human needs

    Science is knowledge of the universe gained by observations and experiments. Technology is the use of this knowledge to help human beings.

(Average) (Skill 28.2)

120. An experiment is performed to determine how the surface area of a liquid affects how long it takes for the liquid to evaporate. One hundred milliliters of water is put in containers with surface areas of 10 cm², 30 cm², 50 cm², 70 cm², and 90 cm². The time it took for each container to evaporate is recorded. Which of the following is a controlled variable?

    A. The time required for each evaporation

    B. The area of the surfaces

    C. The amount of water

    D. The temperature of the water

    Answer: C. The amount of water

    The surface area is the independent variable and the time is the dependent variable. The temperature of the water should have been controlled in this experiment.

(Rigorous) (Skill 28.8)

121. Stars near Earth can be seen to move relative to fixed stars. In observing the motion of a nearby star over a period of decades, an astronomer notices that the path is not a straight line but wobbles about a straight line. The astronomer reports in a peer-reviewed journal that a planet is rotating around the star, causing it to wobble. Which of the following statements best describes the proposition that the star has a planet?

    A. Observation

    B. Hypothesis

    C. Theory

    D. Inference

    Answer: D. Inference

    The observation in the report was the wobbly path of the star. It would be a hypothesis if this was the basis of a further experiment or observation about the existence of the planet. A theory would be more speculative. The astronomer didn't just suggest that the planet was there; the report stated that the star has a planet.

THE ARTS, HEALTH AND PHYSICAL EDUCATION

(Easy) (Skill 43.4)

122. **In order to promote diversity, a teacher should:**

A. Introduce a variety of musical genres

B. Allow students to experiment with all different musical instruments

C. Expose students to various composers

D. All of the above

Answer: D. All of the above

All three choices would ensure that students are being exposed to diversity.

(Average) (Skill 44.1)

123. **Calisthenics develops all of the following health and skill related components of fitness except:**

A. Muscle strength

B. Body composition

C. Power

D. Agility

Answer: C. Power

Calisthenics is a sport that actually helps to keep a body fit in by combining gymnastic and aerobic activities. Calisthenics develop muscle strength and agility and improves body composition. However, calisthenics do not develop power because they do not involve resistance training or explosiveness.

(Average) (Skill 44.12)

124. **Playing "Simon Says" and having students touch different body parts applies which movement concept?**

A. Spatial Awareness

B. Effort Awareness

C. Body Awareness

D. Motion Awareness

Answer: C. Body Awareness

This is a method that integrates European traditions of movement and biomedical knowledge with the East Asian traditions of movement (e.g. Tai chi and Zen meditation).

(Average) (Skill 45.7)

125. **What is the proper sequential order of development for the acquisition of nonlocomotor skills?**

A. Stretch, sit, bend, turn, swing, twist, shake, rock & sway, dodge; fall

B. Bend, stretch, turn, twist, swing, sit, rock & sway, shake, dodge; fall

C. Stretch, bend, sit, shake, turn, rock & sway, swing, twist, dodge; fall

D. Bend, stretch, sit, turn, twist, swing, sway, rock & sway, dodge; fall

Answer: C. Stretch, bend, sit, shake, turn, rock & sway, swing, twist, dodge; fall

Each skill in the progression builds on the previous skills.

(Average) (Skill 44.2)

126. **Which of these is a type of joint?**

    A. Ball and socket

    B. Hinge

    C. Pivot

    D. All of the above

Answer: D. All of the above

A joint is where two bones meet. Joints enable movement. Hinge, ball and socket, and pivot are types of joints.

(Average) (Skill 45.4)

127. **Which movement concept involves students making decisions about an object's positional changes in space?**

    A. Spatial Awareness

    B. Effort Awareness

    C. Body Awareness

    D. Motion Awareness

Answer: A. Spatial Awareness

Spatial awareness is an organized awareness of objects in the space around us. It is also an awareness of our body's position in space. Without this awareness, we would not be able to pick food up from our plates and put it in our mouths. We would have trouble reading, because we could not see the letters in their correct relation to each other and to the page. Athletes would not have the precise awareness of the position of other players on the field and the movement of the ball, which is necessary to play sports effectively.

(Rigorous) (Skill 42.3)

128. **Swimming does not improve which health or skill related component of fitness?**

    A. Cardio-respiratory function

    B. Flexibility

    C. Muscle strength

    D. Foot Speed

Answer: D. Foot Speed

Swimming involves every part of the body. It works on the cardio-respiratory system and it develops flexibility because of the intense body movement in the water. It also improves muscle strength as swimmers must move their bodies against the force of water. Increased foot speed is not an outcome of swimming.

(Average) (Skill 44.14)

129. **The main source of energy comes from?**

    A. Carbohydrates

    B. Water

    C. Protein

    D. Fats

Answer: A. Carbohydrates

Carbohydrates are the main source of energy (glucose) in the human diet. The two types of carbohydrates are simple and complex. Complex carbohydrates have greater nutritional value because they take longer to digest, contain dietary fiber, and do not excessively elevate blood sugar levels. Common sources of carbohydrates are fruits, vegetables, grains, dairy products, and legumes.

(Average) (Skill 45.2)

130. **Which one of these will not help assess current fitness levels and progress?**

    A. Fitnessgram
    B. Pedometers
    C. Presidential Fitness Assessments
    D. Body Mass Index

    Answer: D. Body Mass Index

    Body Mass Index is one method to measure obesity, but it does not give any insight as to what an individual's current fitness levels and progress are.

(Rigorous) (Skill 45.1)

131. **Which is not a benefit of warming up?**

    A. Releasing hydrogen from myoglobin
    B. Reducing the risk of musculoskeletal injuries
    C. Raising the body's core temperature in preparation for activity
    D. Preparing the body for physical activity

    Answer: A. Releasing hydrogen from myoglobin

    Warm-up can reduce the risk of musculoskeletal injuries, raise the body's temperature in preparation for activity, and stretch the major muscle groups. However, a warm-up does not release hydrogen from myoglobin. Myoglobin binds oxygen, not hydrogen.

(Average) (Skill 45.11)

132. **In a physical education classroom, the teacher must:**

    A. Adapt lessons to meet the needs of all learners and included IEP modifications
    B. Only include short term goals to help the student to succeed
    C. Expect the regular education teacher to meet each child's developmental needs
    D. None of the above

    Answer: A. Adapt lessons to meet the needs of all learners and included IEP modifications

    A teacher is responsible for following a student's IEP (Individualized Education Plan) by modifying and adapting lessons and assessments. These include both short and long term goals, and the teacher will most likely work with the regular education teacher to meet the student's needs.

(Easy) (Skill 45.12)

133. **Which of the following is not a manipulative skill?**

    A. Hitting a ball
    B. Jumping rope
    C. Juggling
    D. Skipping

    Answer: D. Skipping

    A manipulative skill is a movement done with another object. Hitting a ball, jumping rope, and juggling are all examples of manipulative skills.

(Easy) (Skill 45.5)

134. **Which of the following is not a category of a movement concept?**

    A. Spacial awareness

    B. Body awareness

    C. Manipulative skills

    D. Locomotor movements

Answer: C. Manipulative Skills

Manipulative skills include hitting, striking, and kicking. Spacial awareness, body awareness, and locomotor movements are all movement concepts.

(Easy) (Skill 43.3)

135. **A music teacher plans an end of the year celebration to conclude the school year. The first grade students she is arranging music for will most likely sing songs that are:**

    A. Largo

    B. Grave

    C. Vivace

    D. None of the above

Answer: C. Vivace

When planning a celebration for young students, music would most likely be upbeat. Vivace describes a tempo that is fast, while Largo and Grave both describe slow paced beats.

(Easy) (Skill 43.3)

136. **After demonstrating her knowledge of the piano and discussing her career with her students, Ms. Bellante, a music teacher:**

    A. Helps students to understand her role within the school system

    B. Allows students to understand ways in which they may be involved in music

    C. Encourages trying new concepts

    D. All of the above

Answer: D. All of the above

All three answers are true. This music teacher would help her students understand her role in the school, ways in which they might become involved in music, and also encourage them to try new concepts.

(Average) (Skill 43.2)

137. **A series of single tones that add up to a recognizable sound is called a:**

    A. Cadence

    B. Rhythm

    C. Melody

    D. Sequence

Answer: C. Melody

A melody is an arrangement of single tones in a meaningful sequence. Cadence is the closing of a phrase or section of music. Rhythm is the regular occurrence of accented beats that shape the character of music or dance.

(Easy)

138. When planning a production, Mr. Garrett's class begins practicing on the stage. He instructs some of his students to wait quietly off to the side of the stage before their parts begin. The place he is referring to is known as:

   A. Upstage
   B. The wings
   C. The legs
   D. The orchestra pit

Answer: B. The wings

This describes the area on stage on each side that is not visible to the audience.

(Average)

139. A teacher assigns her students with the task of moving creatively in a way that expresses a given word. This allows students to:

   A. Understand vocabulary words
   B. Demonstrate creative expression and performance
   C. Promote confidence
   D. All of the above

Answer: D. All of the above

This activity would allow students to understand vocabulary words, demonstrate creative expression and performance, and promote confidence

(Easy) (Skill 46.7)

140. An appropriate theatrical production for young students is:

   A. *West Side Story*
   B. *Peter Pan*
   C. *Macbeth*
   D. *The Lost Colony*

Answer: B. *Peter Pan*

An appropriate production for young learners must be one that focuses on an appropriate topic and can be easily understood. The other choices are appropriate choices for secondary and post-secondary students.

POSTTEST

English Language Arts and Reading

(Easy) (Skill 1.7)

1. To make an inference a reader must:

   A. Make a logical guess as to the next event.
   B. Find a line of reasoning on which to rely.
   C. Make a decision based on an observation.
   D. Use prior knowledge and apply it to the current situation.

(Rigorous) (Skill 7.4)

2. Which of the following is NOT utilized by a reader when trying to comprehend the meaning behind the literal text?

   A. Pictures and graphics in the text
   B. Background knowledge about a topic
   C. Knowledge of different types of text structure
   D. Context clues

(Average) (Skill 2.1)

3. Phonological awareness includes all of the following skills except:

   A. Rhyming and syllabification
   B. Blending sounds into words
   C. Understanding the meaning of the root word
   D. Removing initial sounds and substituting others

(Easy) (Skill 7.5)

4. Asking a child if what he or she has read makes sense to him or her, is prompting the child to use:

   A. Phonics cues
   B. Syntactic cues
   C. Semantic cues
   D. Prior knowledge

(Rigorous) (Skill 6.1)

5. Which of the following indicates that a student is a fluent reader?

   A. Reads texts with expression or prosody
   B. Reads word-to-word and haltingly
   C. Must intentionally decode a majority of the words
   D. In a writing assignment, sentences are poorly-organized, structurally

(Rigorous) (Skill 5.1)

6. If a student has a poor vocabulary the teacher should recommend that:

   A. The student read newspapers, magazines, and books on a regular basis
   B. The student enroll in a Latin class
   C. The student writes the words repetitively after looking them up in the dictionary
   D. The student use a thesaurus to locate synonyms and incorporate them into his/her vocabulary

(Easy) (Skill 5.2)

7. **To decode is to:**
   A. Construct meaning
   B. Sound out a printed sequence of letters
   C. Use a special code to decipher a message
   D. None of the above

(Average) (Skill 6.5)

8. **John Bunyan, Coleridge, Shakespeare, Homer, and Chaucer all contributed to what genre of literature?**
   A. Children's literature
   B. Preadolescent literature
   C. Adolescent literature
   D. Adult literature

(Rigorous) (Skill 8.1)

9. **Which is NOT a true statement concerning informational texts?**
   A. They contain concepts or phenomena
   B. They could explain history
   C. They are based on research
   D. They are presented in a very straightforward, choppy manner

(Rigorous) (Skill 4.4)

10. **Which of the following is NOT true of slant rhyme?**
    A. This occurs when a rhyme is not exact
    B. Words are used to evoke meaning by their sounds
    C. The final consonant sounds are the same, but the vowels are different
    D. It occurs frequently in Welsh verse

(Average) (Skill 8.2)

11. **The literary device of personification is used in which example below?**
    A. "Beg me no beggary by soul or parents, whining dog!"
    B. "Happiness sped through the halls cajoling as it went."
    C. "O wind thy horn, thou proud fellow."
    D. "And that one talent which is death to hide."

(Rigorous) (Skill 8.4)

12. **All of the following are true about graphic organizers EXCEPT:**
    A. Solidify a visual relationship among various reading and writing ideas
    B. Organize information for an advanced reader
    C. Provide scaffolding for instruction
    D. Activate prior knowledge

(Average) (Skill 9.6)

13. **The following words are made plural correctly EXCEPT:**
    A. Radios
    B. Bananas
    C. Poppies
    D. Tomatos

(Rigorous) (Skill 9.7)

14. The following sentences are correct EXCEPT:

    A. One of the boys was playing too rough.

    B. A man and his dog were jogging on the beach.

    C. The House of Representatives has adjourned for the holidays.

    D. Neither Don nor Joyce have missed a day of school this year.

(Rigorous) (Skill 9.8)

15. All of the following are correctly punctuated EXCEPT:

    A. "The airplane crashed on the runway during takeoff."

    B. I was embarrassed when Mrs. White said, "Your slip is showing!"

    C. "The middle school readers were unprepared to understand Bryant's poem 'Thanatopsis.'"

    D. The hall monitor yelled, "Fire! Fire!"

(Average) (Skill 1.2)

16. Students who are learning English as a second language often require which of the following to process new information?

    A. Translators

    B. Reading tutors

    C. Instruction in their native language

    D. Additional time and repetitions

(Rigorous) (Skill 1.3)

17. A student who has difficulty pronouncing certain words or sounds may be demonstrating which speech and language disorder?

    A. Apraxia

    B. Articulation disorder

    C. Auditory processing

    D. Dysarthria

(Rigorous) (Skill 4.7)

18. Identify the type of appeal used by Molly Ivins's in this excerpt from her essay "Get a Knife, Get a Dog, But Get Rid of Guns."

    As a civil libertarian, I, of course, support the Second Amendment. And I believe it means exactly what it says:

    "A well regulated militia being necessary to the security of a free state, the right of the people to keep and bear arms shall not be infringed."

    A. Appeal based on writer's credibility

    B. Appeal to logic

    C. Appeal to the emotion

    D. Appeal to the reader

(Average) (Skill 7.9)

19. "What is the point?" is the first question to be asked when:

    A. Reading a written piece

    B. Listening to a presentation

    C. Writing a composition

    D. All of the above

(Easy) (Skill 10.4)

20. All of the following are true about writing an introduction EXCEPT:

    A. It should be written last

    B. It should lead the audience into the discourse

    C. It is the point of the paper

    D. It can take up a large percentage of the total word count

(Easy) (Skill 1.6)

21. Children typically learn the majority of their words and phrases from:

    A. School

    B. Reading

    C. Peers

    D. Other

(Average) (Skill 9.1)

22. Isaac is mimicking the way his father is writing. He places a piece of paper on the table and holds the pencil in his hand correctly, but he merely draws lines and makes random marks on the paper. What type of writer is he?

    A. Role play writer

    B. Emergent writer

    C. Developing writer

    D. Beginning writer

(Easy) (Skill 3.3)

23. The basic features of the alphabetic principle include:

    A. Students need to be able to take spoken words apart and blend different sounds together to make new words.

    B. Students need to apply letter sounds to all their reading.

    C. The teaching of the alphabetic principle usually begins in kindergarten.

    D. All of the above

(Average) (Skill 10.3)

24. Topic sentences, transition words, and appropriate vocabulary are used by writers to:

    A. Meet various purposes

    B. Organize a multi-paragraph essay

    C. Express an attitude on a subject

    D. Explain the presentation of ideas

(Rigorous) (Skill 10.7)

25. Which of the following should students use to improve coherence of ideas within an argument?

    A. Transitional words or phrases to show relationship of ideas

    B. Conjunctions like "and" to join ideas together

    C. Use direct quotes extensively to improve credibility

    D. Adjectives and adverbs to provide stronger detail

(Rigorous) (Skill 12.11)

26. When giving instructions, all of the following are important stylistic elements EXCEPT:

    A. Present in a serious and friendly tone
    B. Speak clearly and slowly
    C. Note the mood of the audience
    D. Review points of confusion

(Rigorous) (Skill 1.8)

27. When speaking on a formal platform, students should do all of the following EXCEPT:

    A. Use no contractions
    B. Have longer sentences
    C. Connect with the audience
    D. Strictly organize longer segments

(Average) (Skill 1.9)

28. To determine an author's purpose a reader must:

    A. Use his or her own judgment.
    B. Verify all the facts.
    C. Link the causes to the effects.
    D. Rely on common sense.

(Rigorous) (Skill 3.1)

29. Julia has been hired to work in a school that serves a local public housing project. She is working with kindergarten children and has been asked to focus on shared reading. She selects:

    A. Chapter books
    B. Riddle books
    C. Alphabet books
    D. Wordless picture books

(Rigorous) (Skill 3.5)

30. Four of Ms. Wolmark's students have lived in other countries. She is particularly pleased to be studying Sumerian proverbs with them as part of the fifth grade unit in analyzing the sayings of other cultures because:

    A. This gives her a break from teaching, and the children can share sayings from other cultures they and their families have experienced
    B. This validates the experiences and expertise of ELL learners in her classroom
    C. This provides her children from the U.S. with a lens on other cultural values
    D. All of the above

(Average) (Skill 7.2)

31. Which of the following is an important feature of vocabulary instruction, according to the National Reading Panel?

    A. Repetition of vocabulary items
    B. Keeping a consistent task structure at all times
    C. Teaching vocabulary in more than one language
    D. Isolating vocabulary instruction from other subjects

(Rigorous) (Skill 10.6)

32. Exposition occurs within a story:

    A. After the rising action
    B. After the denouement
    C. Before the rising action
    D. Before the setting

(Easy) (Skill 1.5)

33. The idea that students need to be able to take spoken words apart and blend different sounds together to make words describes:

   A. The alphabetic principle
   B. Syntax
   C. Phonics
   D. Morphology

(Easy) (Skill 3.2)

34. Which of the following strategies encourages print awareness in classrooms?

   A. Word walls
   B. Using big books to read to students
   C. Using highlighters to locate uppercase letters
   D. All of the above

(Easy) (Skill 4.5)

35. Teaching students how to interpret _____ involves evaluating a text's headings, subheadings, bolded words, and side notes.

   A. graphic organizers
   B. text structure
   C. textual marking
   D. summaries

(Average) (Skill 6.3)

36. The complex linguistic deficiency marked by the inability to remember and recognize words by sounds and, further, the inability to break words down into component units describes:

   A. Oral processing disorder
   B. Attention deficit disorder
   C. Dyslexia
   D. None of the above

(Rigorous) (Skill 6.4)

37. Academically, appropriate literature primarily helps students to _____.

   A. become better readers
   B. see how the skills they learned are applied to writing
   C. enjoy library time
   D. increase academic skills in other content areas

(Average) (Skill 9.3)

38. Which of the following is NOT an effective strategy to aid students with spelling instruction?

   A. Knowledge of patterns, sounds, and letter-sound association
   B. Memorizing sight words
   C. Writing words one or two times
   D. Writing the words correctly in personal writing

(Rigorous) (Skill 9.1)

39. Which number order below displays the appropriate sequence for developing writing skills?

    1. Experimental writing
    2. Early writing
    3. Role-play writing
    4. Conventional writing

    A. 1, 4, 2, 3
    B. 3, 1, 2, 4
    C. 3, 2, 1, 4
    D. 1, 2, 4, 3

(Rigorous) (Skill 9.3)

40. In the _____ stage of writing, students write in scribbles and can assign meaning to the markings.

    A. role-play writing
    B. experimental writing
    C. early writing
    D. conventional writing

MATH

(Average) (Skill 14.1)

41. Which of the following statements best characterizes the meaning of "absolute value of x"?

    A. The square root of x
    B. The square of x
    C. The distance on a number line between x and $-x$
    D. The distance on a number line between 0 and x

(Average) (Skill 14.2)

42. Which number is equivalent to the following expression?

    $3 \times 10^3 + 9 \times 10^0 + 6 + 10^{-2} + 8 \times 10^{-3}$

    A. 3,900.68
    B. 3,009.068
    C. 39.68
    D. 309.068

(Average) (Skill 14.5)

43. Which of the following terms most accurately describes the set of numbers below?

    $\{3, \sqrt{16}, \pi^0, 6, \frac{28}{4}\}$

    A. Rationals
    B. Irrationals
    C. Complex
    D. Whole numbers

(Average) (Skill 14.7)

44. Calculate the value of the following expression.

    $\left(\frac{6}{3} + 1 \cdot 5\right)^2 \cdot \frac{1}{7} + (3 \cdot 2 - 1)$

    A. 6
    B. 10
    C. 12
    D. 294

(Rigorous) (Skill 14.8)

45. What is the GCF of 12, 30, 56, and 144?

    A. 2
    B. 3
    C. 5
    D. 7

(Rigorous) (Skill 13.9)

46. In a certain classroom, 32% of the students are male. What is the minimum number of females in the class?

   A. 68
   B. 34
   C. 32
   D. 17

(Average) (Skill 13.2)

47. The final cost of an item (with sales tax) is $8.35. If the sales tax is 7%, what was the pre-tax price of the item?

   A. $7.80
   B. $8.00
   C. $8.28
   D. $8.93

(Average) (Skill 16.9)

48. A traveler uses a ruler and finds the distance between two cities to be 3.5 inches. If the legend indicates that 100 miles is the same as an inch, what is the distance in miles between the cities?

   A. 29 miles
   B. 35 miles
   C. 100 miles
   D. 350 miles

(Average) (Skill 15.7)

49. A burning candle loses $\frac{1}{2}$ inch in height every hour. If the original height of the candle was 6 inches, which of the following equations describes the relationship between the height h of the candle and the number of hours t since it was lit?

   A. $2h + t = 12$
   B. $2h - t = 12$
   C. $h = 6 - t$
   D. $h = 0.5t + 6$

(Average) (Skill 15.1)

50. Three less than four times a number is five times the sum of that number and 6. Which equation could be used to solve this problem?

   A. $3 - 4n = 5(n + 6)$
   B. $3 - 4n + 5n = 6$
   C. $4n - 3 = 5n + 6$
   D. $4n - 3 = 5(n + 6)$

(Rigorous) (Skill 15.4)

51. Which set is closed under addition?

   A. $\{0, \frac{1}{2}, \frac{1}{4}, \frac{1}{8}, \frac{1}{16}, \ldots\}$
   B. $\{\ldots, -2, -1, 0, 1, 2, \ldots\}$
   C. $\{-1, 0, 1\}$
   D. $\{0, 1, 2, 3, 4, 5\}$

(Average) (Skill 15.2)

52. Which property justifies the following manipulation?

    $x^2 - 3y \rightarrow 3y + x^2$

    A. Associative
    B. Commutative
    C. Distributive
    D. None of the above

(Rigorous) (Skill 15.6)

53. Which set cannot be considered "dense"?

    A. Integers
    B. Rationals
    C. Irrationals
    D. Reals

(Average) (Skill 15.3)

54. Which of the following is an example of a multiplicative inverse?

    A. $x^2 - x^2 = 0$
    B. $(y - 3)^0 = 1$
    C. $\frac{1}{e^{3z}} = 1$
    D. $f^2 = \frac{1}{g}$

(Rigorous) (Skill 15.10)

55. Two farmers are buying feed for animals. One farmer buys eight bags of grain and six bales of hay for $105, and the other farmer buys three bags of grain and nine bales of hay for $69.75. How much is a bag of grain?

    A. $4.50
    B. $9.75
    C. $14.25
    D. $28.50

(Rigorous) (Skill 15.9)

56. Which expression best characterizes the shaded area in the graph below?

    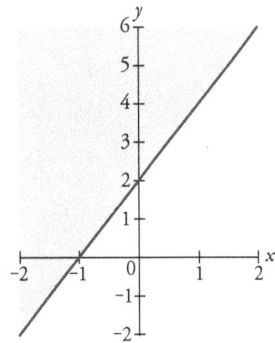

    A. $y \leq -x + 2$
    B. $y \geq 2x + 2$
    C. $y = 2x + 2$
    D. $y \geq 2x - 1$

(Rigorous) (Skill 15.5)

57. Solve for L:

    $R = r + \frac{400(W - L)}{N}$

    A. $L = W - \frac{N}{400}(R - r)$
    B. $L = W + \frac{N}{400}(R - r)$
    C. $L = W - \frac{400}{N}(R - r)$
    D. $L = \frac{NR}{r} = 400W$

(Rigorous) (Skill 16.2)

58. The formula for the volume of a cylinder is $V = \pi r^2 h$ where r is the radius of the cylinder and h is its height. What is the volume of a cylinder of diameter 2 cm and height 5 cm?

    A. 25π cm^2
    B. 5π cm^2
    C. 20π cm^2
    D. 50π cm^2

(Rigorous) (Skill 16.7)

59. The figure below is an equilateral triangle. Which transformation converts the solid-line figure to the broken-line figure?

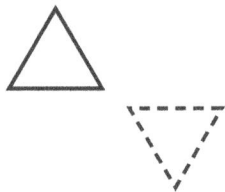

A. Rotation
B. Reflection
C. Glide reflection
D. Any of the above

(Rigorous) (Skill 16.6)

60. Which of the following is a net of a cube?

A.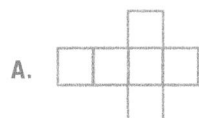

B.

C.

D.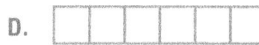

(Rigorous) (Skill 16.3)

61. What is the length of the shortest side of a right isosceles triangle if the longest side is 5 centimeters?

A. 2.24 centimeters
B. 2.5 centimeters
C. 3.54 centimeters
D. Not enough information

(Average) (Skill 16.4)

62. What is the area of the shaded region below, where the circle has a radius r?

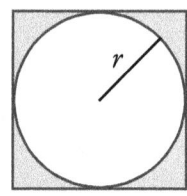

A. r^2
B. $(4 - \pi)r^2$
C. $(2 - \pi)r^2$
D. $4\pi r^2$

(Average) (Skill 16.8)

63. The figure below is constructed with congruent equilateral triangles each having sides of length 4 units. What is the perimeter of the figure?

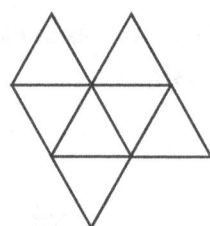

A. 9 units
B. 36 units
C. 60 units
D. Not enough information

QUESTIONS

(Average) (Skill 17.2)

64. The following stem and leaf plot shows rainfall data in inches over several consecutive days. What is the median value?

0	7
1	3 9
2	1 5 7 8
3	0 3 4 6 6 9
4	3 5 5 7 8
5	0 0 3 5
10	3

A. 3.6 in
B. 3.9 in
C. 4.3 in
D. 3.4 in

(Rigorous) (Skill 17.4)

65. A bag contains four red marbles and six blue marbles. If three selections are made without replacement, what is the probability of choosing three red marbles?

A. $\frac{3}{10}$
B. $\frac{8}{125}$
C. $\frac{1}{30}$
D. $\frac{1}{60}$

(Average) (Skill 17.3)

66. What is the sample space for the sum of the outcomes for two rolls of a six-sided die?

A. {1, 2, 3, 4, 5, 6}
B. {1, 2, 3, 4, 5, 6, 7, 8, 9, 10, 11, 12}
C. {2, 3, 4, 5, 6, 7, 8, 9, 10, 11, 12}
D. {7, 8, 9, 10, 11, 12}

(Rigorous) (Skill 17.5)

67. How many different three-card hands can be drawn from a standard deck of 52 playing cards?

A. 156
B. 2,704
C. 132,600
D. 140,608

(Rigorous) (Skill 14.5)

68. The number "0" is a member of all of the following groups of numbers EXCEPT:

A. Whole numbers
B. Real numbers
C. Natural numbers
D. Integers

(Rigorous) (Skill 13.8)

69. Students in Mr. Anderson's class want to know which train car will hold more plastic apples: the long, thin car, or the square car. First, they fill the long, thin car with apples and record their answer. Then they fill the square car with apples and record their answer. Which math principles does this activity demonstrate?

A. Problem solving, subtraction
B. Subtraction, meaningful counting
C. Problem solving, number sense
D. Addition, problem solving

TEACHER CERTIFICATION STUDY GUIDE

(Easy) (Skill 16.4)

70. In a _____ all sides are the same length and all angles are the same measure.

    A. triangle

    B. regular polygon

    C. sphere

    D. parallelogram

(Easy) (Skill 16.7)

71. Which letter does not demonstrate symmetry?

    A. T

    B. A

    C. O

    D. F

(Rigorous) (Skill 18.9)

72. Which types of graphs would best be used to represent the number of students who like red, green, or yellow best?

    A. A bar graph or pictograph

    B. A pictograph or line graph

    C. A stem and leaf plot or bar graph

    D. A line graph or stem and leaf plot

(Rigorous) (Skill 18.1)

73. Students in a kindergarten class are curious about which toy is heavier: a plastic doll or a metal truck. They use a balance and wooden cubes to determine their answer. The toy that requires more cubes to hold the balance even will be the heavier toy. Which math principles does this activity demonstrate?

    A. Subtraction, meaningful counting

    B. Problem solving, number sense

    C. Addition, problem solving

    D. Problem solving, subtraction

SOCIAL SCIENCES

(Average) (Skill 21.2)

74. Denver is called the "mile-high city" because it is:

    A. Located approximately one mile above the plains of eastern Colorado

    B. Located exactly one mile above the base of Cheyenne Mountain

    C. Located approximately one mile above sea level

    D. The city with the tallest buildings in Colorado

(Rigorous) (Skill 21.3)

75. The state of Louisiana is divided into parishes. What type of region do the parishes represent?

    A. Formal region

    B. Functional region

    C. Vernacular region

    D. Human region

(Average) (Skill 21.1)

76. Which continent is only one country?

   A. Australia
   B. New Zealand
   C. The Arctic
   D. Antarctica

(Rigorous) (Skill 19.10)

77. The Southern Hemisphere contains all of which continent?

   A. Africa
   B. Australia
   C. South America
   D. North America

(Average) (Skill 20.2)

78. Anthropology is:

   A. The profession that made the Leakey family famous
   B. The scientific study of human culture and humanity
   C. Not related to geography at all
   D. Margaret Mead's study of the Samoans

(Rigorous) (Skill 21.8)

79. In the 1920s, Margaret Mead wrote *Coming of Age in Samoa,* relating her observations about this group's way of life. What of these types of geographical study best describes her method?

   A. Regional
   B. Topical
   C. Physical
   D. Human

(Rigorous) (Skill 21.26)

80. Which activity is most likely to have a negative environmental impact on an area?

   I. Building a new skyscraper in Manhattan
   II. Strip mining for coal in West Virginia
   III. Digging a new oil well within an existing oilfield in Texas
   IV. Building ten new homes in a 100-acre suburban neighborhood that already contains fifty homes

   A. II and III only
   B. II only
   C. I only
   D. I and IV only

(Average) (Skill 22.2)

81. Which of the following are two agricultural innovations that began in China?

   A. Using pesticides and fertilizer
   B. Irrigation and cuneiform
   C. Improving the silk industry and inventing gunpowder
   D. Terrace farming and crop rotation

(Average) (Skill 21.21)

82. Which civilization laid the foundations of geometry?

   A. Egyptian
   B. Greek
   C. Roman
   D. Chinese

(Average) (Skill 20.8)

83. The international organization established to work for world peace at the end of the Second World War is the:

   A. League of Nations
   B. United Federation of Nations
   C. United Nations
   D. United World League

(Rigorous) (Skill 23.10)

84. In December, Ms. Griffin asks her students to talk about their holiday traditions. Rebecca explains about lighting the nine candles during Chanukkah, Josh explains about the lighting of the seven candles during Kwanzaa, and Bernard explains about lighting the four candles during Advent. This is an example of:

   A. Cultural diffusion
   B. Cultural identity
   C. Cross-cultural exchanges
   D. Cosmopolitanism

(Average) (Skill 21.10)

85. English and Spanish colonists took what from Native Americans?

   A. Land
   B. Water rights
   C. Money
   D. Religious beliefs

(Average) (Skill 20.4)

86. Spanish colonies were:

   A. Mainly in the northeast
   B. Mainly in the south
   C. Mainly in the Midwest
   D. Mainly in Canada

(Rigorous) (Skill 20.18)

87. In the events leading up to the American Revolution, which of these methods was effective in dealing with the British taxes?

   A. Boycotts
   B. Strikes
   C. Armed conflicts
   D. Resolutions

(Rigorous) (Skill 20.16)

88. One of the political parties that developed in the early 1790s was led by:

   A. Thomas Jefferson
   B. George Washington
   C. Aaron Burr
   D. John Quincy Adams

(Easy) (Skill 20.20)

89. How did the labor force change after 1830?

   A. Employers began using children
   B. Employers began hiring immigrants
   C. Employers began hiring women
   D. Employers began hiring non-immigrant men

(Rigorous) (Skill 20.22)
90. Which of these was not a result of World War I in the United States?

   A. Establishment of new labor laws
   B. Prosperous industrial growth
   C. Formation of the United Nations
   D. Growth of the stock market

(Average) (Skill 23.1)
91. Among civilized people:

   A. Strong government is not necessary
   B. Systems of control are rudimentary at best
   C. Government has no sympathy for individuals or for individual happiness
   D. Governments began to assume more institutional forms

(Rigorous) (Skill 23.2)
92. The U.S. House of Representatives has:

   A. 100 members
   B. 435 members
   C. Three branches
   D. A president and a vice president

(Rigorous) (Skill 23.5)
93. Socialism is:

   A. A system of government with a legislature
   B. A system where the government is subject to a vote of "no confidence"
   C. A political belief and system in which the state takes a guiding role in the national economy
   D. A system of government with three distinct branches

(Average) (Skill 23.3)
94. Which of the following was not a source of conflict in writing the U.S. Constitution?

   A. Establishing a monarchy
   B. Equalizing power between the small states and the large states
   C. Dealing with slavery
   D. Electing a president

(Rigorous) (Skill 23.8)
95. Upon arrest, a person is read a "Miranda warning" which reads, in part, "You have the right to remain silent. Anything you say can and will be used against you in a court of law." Under what amendment in the Bill of Rights is this covered?

   A. The right against unreasonable search and seizures
   B. The right to trial by jury and right to legal council
   C. The right against self-incrimination
   D. The right to jury trial for civil actions

(Rigorous) (Skill 22.5)
96. The equilibrium price:

   A. Is the price that clears the markets
   B. Is the price in the middle
   C. Identifies a shortage or a surplus
   D. Is an agricultural price support

(Rigorous) (Skill 22.6)

97. Capital is:

   A. Anyone who sells his or her ability to produce goods and services

   B. The ability of an individual to combine the three inputs with his or her own talents to produce a viable good or service

   C. Anything that is manufactured to be used in the production process

   D. The land itself and everything occurring naturally on it

(Rigorous) (Skill 22.3)

98. Which of the following countries has historically operated in a market economy?

   A. Great Britain

   B. Cuba

   C. Yugoslavia

   D. India

(Average) (Skill 19.7)

99. For their research paper on the use of technology in the classroom, students have gathered data that shows a sharp increase in the number of online summer classes over the past five years. What would be the best way for them to depict this information visually?

   A. A line chart

   B. A table

   C. A pie chart

   D. A flow chart

(Average) (Skill 19.14)

100. An example of something that is not a primary source is:

   A. The published correspondence between Winston Churchill and Franklin D. Roosevelt during World War II

   B. Martin Gilbert's biography of Winston Churchill

   C. The diary of Field Marshal Sir Alan Brooke, the head of the British Army during World War II

   D. Franklin D. Roosevelt's handwritten notes from the World War II era

(Rigorous) (Skill 19.4)

101. Mr. Phillips is creating a unit to study *To Kill a Mockingbird* and wants to familiarize his high school freshmen with the attitudes and issues of the historical period. Which activity would familiarize students with the attitudes and issues of the Depression-era South?

   A. Create a detailed timeline of 15–20 social, cultural, and political events that focus on race relations in the 1930s

   B. Research and report on the life of its author Harper Lee; compare her background with the events in the book

   C. Watch the movie version and note language and dress

   D. Write a research report on the stock market crash of 1929 and its effects

(Rigorous) (Skill 19.12)

102. Which of the following is NOT an excellent way to teach students about World War II?

   A. To ask a World War II veteran to visit your class and talk to students about the war

B. To have students read books on World War II

C. To have students read primary source materials on World War II, such as the text of the Atlantic Charter

D. To have students watch the movie *Schindler's List*

(Average) (Skill 20.23)

103. What event triggered World War I?

A. The fall of the Weimar Republic

B. The resignation of the czar

C. The assassination of Austrian Archduke Ferdinand

D. The assassination of the czar

(Rigorous) (Skill 22.7)

104. Which one of the following would NOT be considered a result of World War II?

A. Economic depressions and slow resumption of trade and financial aid

B. Western Europe was no longer the center of world power

C. The beginnings of new power struggles, not only in Europe but in Asia as well

D. Territorial and boundary changes for many nations, especially in Europe

SCIENCE

(Easy) (Skill 38.1)

105. Which of the following layers comprises the earth's plates?

A. Mesosphere

B. Troposphere

C. Asthensophere

D. Lithosphere

(Rigorous) (Skill 31.2)

106. What conditions are required to create coarse-grained igneous rocks?

A. High temperature and pressure

B. Slowly cooling magma

C. Quickly cooling lava

D. Evaporation and cementation

(Easy) (Skill 39.5)

107. Which of the following describes the law of superposition?

A. The present is the key to the past

B. The oldest rocks in a rock unit are found on the top of the rock column

C. The oldest rocks in a rock unit are found on the bottom of the rock column

D. Faults that cut across rock units are younger than the units they cut across

(Average) (Skill 39.1)
108. **How are igneous, metamorphic, and sedimentary rocks classified?**
    A. The chemical composition of the rocks
    B. When the rocks were formed
    C. How the rocks were formed
    D. The location of the rocks within the Earth's crust

(Easy) (Skill 34.1)
109. **In which period did land animals first appear?**
    A. 350 to 135 million years ago
    B. Devonian
    C. Paleozoic
    D. Cretaceous

(Easy) (Skill 37.2)
110. **Which era had dinosaurs in it?**
    A. Cenozoic
    B. Mesozoic
    C. Triassic
    D. Paleozoic

(Average) (Skill 41.1)
111. **Which of the following objects in the universe is the largest?**
    A. Pulsars
    B. Quasars
    C. Black holes
    D. Nebulas

(Average) (Skill 38.4)
112. **Why is the northern winter slightly warmer than the southern winter?**
    A. Because the perihelion occurs in January
    B. Because of global warming
    C. Because there is more water in the southern hemisphere
    D. Because Earth rotates on an axis that is not perpendicular to the plane of rotation

(Easy) (Skill 34.4)
113. **What are ribosomes?**
    A. Contain digestive enzymes that break down food
    B. Where proteins are synthesized
    C. Make ATP
    D. Hold stored food

(Easy) (Skill 34.5)
114. **The role of rough endoplasmic reticulum is:**
    A. Metabolic functions
    B. Produce lipids
    C. Produce enzymes
    D. Protein synthesis

(Rigorous) (Skill 35.1)
115. **What is the purpose of sexual reproduction?**
    A. Produce more organisms
    B. Produce organisms that are genetically diverse
    C. Give organisms the protection of male and female parents
    D. Increase social cooperation between organisms

(Average) (Skill 34.2)

116. **In mitotic cell division, at what stage do the chromosomes line up in the cell?**

    A. Interphase

    B. Anaphase

    C. Prophase

    D. Metaphase

(Easy) (Skill 36.3)

117. **According to natural selection:**

    A. Individuals within a population are identical

    B. Those with better traits have less offspring

    C. Successive generations will possess better traits

    D. Single individuals evolve to fit their surroundings

(Easy) (Skill 37.7)

118. **Chemicals released by an organism as way of communicating are called:**

    A. Pheromones

    B. Synapses

    C. Chemoreceptors

    D. Thermoreceptors

(Average) (Skill 37.3)

119. **Which of the following is not a kingdom in the classification of living organisms?**

    A. Plants

    B. Fungi

    C. Viruses

    D. Bacteria

(Average) (Skill 34.3)

120. **Which property do plants have that fungi do not have?**

    A. Sexual reproduction

    B. Photosynthesis

    C. Digestion

    D. Locomotion

(Rigorous) (Skill 35.2)

121. **Which term describes the relationship between barnacles and whales?**

    A. Commensalism

    B. Parasitism

    C. Competition

    D. Mutualism

(Average) (Skill 31.1)

122. **Which of the following describes the transformation of liquid water to ice?**

    A. Chemical change

    B. Physical change

    C. Thermodynamic change

    D. Non-chemical molecular change

(Average) (Skill 32.1)

123. **Will Lithium gain or lose an electron when forming an ion? How many electrons will it gain or lose?**

    A. Gain 1

    B. Gain 2

    C. Lose 1

    D. Lose 2

(Rigorous) (Skill 30.4)

124. On which of the following does the force of friction between a metal stool and a wooden floor NOT depend?

   A. The speed of the chair
   B. Whether the stool has three legs or four
   C. The type of metal
   D. The smoothness of the floor

(Easy) (Skill 30.1)

125. Which of the following laws implies that the force on an object comes from another object?

   A. Newton's first law of motion
   B. Newton's second law of motion
   C. Newton's third law of motion
   D. Coulomb's law

(Easy) (Skill 32.2)

126. Which of the following quantities has the units of calories per degree?

   A. Heat capacity
   B. Specific heat
   C. Heat equivalent
   D. Heat transfer

(Easy) (Skill 27.1)

127. A controlled experiment with tomato plants was conducted to see if the amount of water given to the plants affected the number of tomatoes grown. One plant was given 1 gallon of water, another 2 gallons, another 3 gallons, etc. The number of tomatoes produced for each plant was measured. What was the controlled variable?

   A. Type of plant
   B. Amount of water
   C. Number of tomatoes
   D. Amount of fertilizer

(Easy) (Skill 25.1)

128. Which of the following should be limited in a balanced diet?

   A. Carbohydrates
   B. Fats and oils
   C. Proteins
   D. Vitamins

(Average) (Skill 25.1)

129. Which of the following statements about scientific knowledge best explains what scientific knowledge is?

   A. Scientific knowledge is based on experiments
   B. Science knowledge is empirical
   C. Scientific knowledge is tentative
   D. Scientific knowledge is based on reason

(Average) (Skill 25.5)

130. An experiment is performed to determine the effects of acid rain on plant life. Which of the following would be the variable?

    A. The type of plant
    B. The amount of light
    C. The pH of the water
    D. The amount of water

(Average) (Skill 44.1)

131. Calisthenics develops all of the following health and skill related components of fitness except:

    A. Muscle strength
    B. Body composition
    C. Power
    D. Agility

(Easy) (Skill 44.2)

132. Which of the following should be limited in a balanced diet?

    A. Carbohydrates
    B. Fats and oils
    C. Proteins
    D. Vitamins

(Average) (Skill 45.8)

133. Which type of physical education activity would be most likely to help students develop a sense of belonging?

    A. Solitary activities
    B. Teamwork activities
    C. Competitive activities
    D. Creative activities

(Average) (Skill 45.1)

134. Which of the following help children to develop fine and gross motor skills?

    A. Tearing newspaper into strips
    B. Cutting pictures from magazines
    C. Manipulating play dough
    D. All of the above

(Average) (Skill 45.10)

135. Which of the following activities incorporates physical science with physical education?

    A. Analyzing how runners can reduce friction
    B. Studying the use of statistics in sport
    C. Researching how athletes use sports psychology
    D. Considering the biochemistry of producing energy

(Average) (Skill 45.12)

136. The teaching of sports psychology incorporates physical education with _____.

    A. physical science
    B. natural science
    C. mathematics
    D. social science

(Easy) (Skill 45.4)

137. Which of the following benefits can physical education provide?

    A. A sense of belonging
    B. Increased self-esteem
    C. Appreciation of beauty
    D. All of the above

(Average) (Skill 45.7)

138. Which locomotor skill is a game of Fox and Hound most likely to be used to develop?

    A. Creeping

    B. Hopping

    C. Galloping

    D. Leaping

(Easy) (Skill 43.2)

139. Which subject would be most likely to develop a student's body awareness and listening skills?

    A. Visual arts

    B. Dance

    C. Drama

    D. Music

(Easy) (Skill 43.1)

140. Which of the following is considered the universal language?

    A. Math

    B. History

    C. Music

    D. Art

ANSWER KEY AND RIGOR TABLE

Posttest Answer Key

1. D	15. B	29. D	43. D	57. A	71. D	85. A	99. A	113. B	127. A
2. A	16. D	30. D	44. C	58. B	72. A	86. B	100. B	114. D	128. B
3. C	17. B	31. A	45. A	59. D	73. B	87. A	101. A	115. B	129. B
4. C	18. A	32. C	46. D	60. A	74. C	88. A	102. D	116. D	130. C
5. A	19. D	33. A	47. A	61. C	75. A	89. B	103. C	117. C	131. C
6. A	20. C	34. D	48. D	62. B	76. A	90. C	104. A	118. A	132. A
7. B	21. B	35. B	49. A	63. B	77. B	91. D	105. D	119. C	133. B
8. D	22. A	36. C	50. D	64. B	78. B	92. B	106. B	120. B	134. D
9. D	23. D	37. B	51. B	65. C	79. D	93. C	107. C	121. A	135. A
10. B	24. B	38. C	52. B	66. C	80. B	94. A	108. C	122. B	136. D
11. B	25. A	39. B	53. A	67. C	81. D	95. C	109. B	123. C	137. D
12. B	26. A	40. A	54. C	68. C	82. B	96. A	110. B	124. B	138. C
13. D	27. C	41. D	55. B	69. C	83. C	97. C	111. B	125. C	139. B
14. D	28. A	42. B	56. B	70. B	84. C	98. A	112. A	126. A	140. C

Posttest Rigor Table

Easy 20%	1, 4, 7, 20, 21, 23, 33, 34, 35, 70, 71, 89, 105, 107, 109, 110, 113, 114, 117, 118, 125, 126, 127, 128, 132, 137, 139, 140
Average 40%	3, 8, 11, 13, 16, 19, 22, 24, 28, 31, 36, 38, 41, 42, 43, 49, 50, 52, 54, 62, 63, 64, 66, 74, 76, 78, 81, 82, 83, 91, 92, 94, 99, 100, 103, 108, 111, 112, 116, 119, 120, 122, 123, 129, 130, 131, 133, 134, 135, 136, 138
Rigorous 40%	2, 5, 6, 9, 10, 12, 14, 15, 17, 18, 25, 26, 27, 29, 30, 32, 37, 39, 40, 45, 46, 51, 53, 55, 56, 57, 60, 61, 65, 67, 68, 69, 72, 73, 75, 77, 79, 80, 84, 87, 88, 90, 93, 95, 96, 97, 98, 101, 102, 104, 106, 115, 121, 124

POSTTEST WITH RATIONALES

English Language Arts and Reading

(Easy) (Skill 1.7)

1. **To make an inference a reader must:**
   A. Make a logical guess as to the next event.
   B. Find a line of reasoning on which to rely.
   C. Make a decision based on an observation.
   D. Use prior knowledge and apply it to the current situation.

   Answer: D. Use prior knowledge and apply it to the current situation.

   Prior knowledge applied to the situation at hand is essential in making a valid inference. Because choices A–C do not involve prior knowledge, they are not correct ways to make an inference.

(Rigorous) (Skill 7.4)

2. **Which of the following is NOT utilized by a reader when trying to comprehend the meaning behind the literal text?**
   A. Pictures and graphics in the text
   B. Background knowledge about a topic
   C. Knowledge of different types of text structure
   D. Context clues

   Answer: A. Pictures and graphics in the text

   While pictures and graphics can be helpful, good readers are trying to extract meaning from the text itself by comparing new information to background knowledge, using knowledge of a type of text to build expectations, and making use of context clues to help identify unknown words.

(Average) (Skill 2.1)

3. **Phonological awareness includes all of the following skills except:**
   A. Rhyming and syllabification
   B. Blending sounds into words
   C. Understanding the meaning of the root word
   D. Removing initial sounds and substituting others

   Answer: C. Understanding the meaning of the root word

   Phonological awareness involves the recognition that spoken words are composed of a set of smaller units such as onsets and rhymes, syllables, and sounds.

(Easy) (Skill 7.5)

4. **Asking a child if what he or she has read makes sense to him or her, is prompting the child to use:**
   A. Phonics cues
   B. Syntactic cues
   C. Semantic cues
   D. Prior knowledge

   Answer: C. Semantic cues

Children use their prior knowledge, sense of the story, and pictures to support their predicting and confirming the meaning of the text.

(Rigorous) (Skill 6.1)

5. **Which of the following indicates that a student is a fluent reader?**

   A. Reads texts with expression or prosody
   B. Reads word-to-word and haltingly
   C. Must intentionally decode a majority of the words
   D. In a writing assignment, sentences are poorly-organized, structurally

   Answer: A. Reads texts with expression or prosody

   The teacher should listen to the children read aloud, but there are also clues to reading levels in their writing.

(Rigorous) (Skill 5.1)

6. **If a student has a poor vocabulary the teacher should recommend that:**

   A. The student read newspapers, magazines, and books on a regular basis
   B. The student enroll in a Latin class
   C. The student writes the words repetitively after looking them up in the dictionary
   D. The student use a thesaurus to locate synonyms and incorporate them into his/her vocabulary

   Answer: A. The student read newspapers, magazines, and books on a regular basis

   It is up to the teacher to help the student choose reading material, but the student must be able to choose where s/he will search for the reading pleasure indispensable for enriching vocabulary.

(Easy) (Skill 5.2)

7. **To decode is to:**

   A. Construct meaning
   B. Sound out a printed sequence of letters
   C. Use a special code to decipher a message
   D. None of the above

   Answer: B. Sound out a printed sequence of letters

   To decode means to change communication signals into messages. Reading comprehension requires that the reader learn the code within which a message is written and be able to decode it to get the message.

(Average) (Skill 6.5)

8. **John Bunyan, Coleridge, Shakespeare, Homer, and Chaucer all contributed to what genre of literature?**

   A. Children's literature
   B. Preadolescent literature
   C. Adolescent literature
   D. Adult literature

   Answer: D. Adult literature

   These five authors contributed to the adult literature genre as they were authoring titles before children's and pre-adolescent/adolescent literature became recognized as separate genres that authors purposefully contributed towards.

POSTTEST

(Rigorous) (Skill 8.1)

9. Which is NOT a true statement concerning informational texts?

   A. They contain concepts or phenomena
   B. They could explain history
   C. They are based on research
   D. They are presented in a very straightforward, choppy manner

Answer: D. They are presented in a very straightforward, choppy manner

Informational texts are types of books that explain concepts or phenomena like history or the idea of photosynthesis. Informational texts are usually based on research. Texts that are presented in a very straightforward or choppy manner are newspaper articles.

(Rigorous) (Skill 4.4)

10. Which of the following is NOT true of slant rhyme?

    A. This occurs when a rhyme is not exact
    B. Words are used to evoke meaning by their sounds
    C. The final consonant sounds are the same, but the vowels are different
    D. It occurs frequently in Welsh verse

Answer: B. Words are used to evoke meaning by their sounds

Slant rhyme occurs when a rhyme is not exact because the final consonant sounds may be the same while the vowel sounds are different. Examples include: "green" and "gone" or "that" and "hit." This type of device occurs frequently in Welsh verse as well as in Irish and Icelandic verse. Poets who use words to evoke meaning by their sounds are using onomatopoeia.

(Average) (Skill 8.2)

11. The literary device of personification is used in which example below?

    A. "Beg me no beggary by soul or parents, whining dog!"
    B. "Happiness sped through the halls cajoling as it went."
    C. "O wind thy horn, thou proud fellow."
    D. "And that one talent which is death to hide."

Answer: B. "Happiness sped through the halls cajoling as it went."

The correct answer is B. Personification is defined as giving human characteristics to inanimate objects or concepts. It can be thought of as a sub-category of metaphor. Happiness, an abstract concept, is "speeding through the halls" and "cajoling," both of which are human behaviors, so happiness is being compared to a human being. Choice A is figurative and metaphorical but not a personification. Choice C is, again, figurative and metaphorical but not a personification. The speaker is, perhaps, telling someone that they are bragging, or "blowing their own horn." Choice D is also figurative and metaphorical but not personification. Hiding a particular talent is being compared to risking death.

(Rigorous) (Skill 8.4)

12. **All of the following are true about graphic organizers EXCEPT:**

    A. Solidify a visual relationship among various reading and writing ideas

    B. Organize information for an advanced reader

    C. Provide scaffolding for instruction

    D. Activate prior knowledge

Answer: B. Organize information for an advanced reader

A graphic organizer is a tool that students can use to help them visualize ideas in a text. They are also a helpful scaffolding tool as they help students activate their prior knowledge on the topic at hand. Choice B is incorrect because graphic organizers are relevant tools for young and/or basic readers and are not just for the advanced or independent.

(Average) (Skill 9.6)

13. **The following words are made plural correctly EXCEPT:**

    A. Radios

    B. Bananas

    C. Poppies

    D. Tomatos

Answer: D. Tomatos

Words that end in *o* with a consonant before it require adding an *es* for the plural form. *Radio* does not have a consonant before the *o* and therefore only takes the *s* ending to avoid three vowels in a row.

(Rigorous) (Skill 9.7)

14. **The following sentences are correct EXCEPT:**

    A. One of the boys was playing too rough.

    B. A man and his dog were jogging on the beach.

    C. The House of Representatives has adjourned for the holidays.

    D. Neither Don nor Joyce have missed a day of school this year.

Answer: D. Neither Don nor Joyce have missed a day of school this year.

A verb should always agree in number with its subject. Making them agree requires the ability to locate the subject of a sentence. In choice A the subject, one, is singular and requires a singular verb. In choice B the subject, man and dog, is plural and requires a plural verb, In choice C the subject, House of Representatives, is collectively singular and requires a singular verb. In choice D the subject, Don and Joyce, are both singular and connected by nor which requires the use of a singular verb, and "have" is plural and therefore incorrect.

(Rigorous) (Skill 9.8)

15. **All of the following are correctly punctuated EXCEPT:**

    A. "The airplane crashed on the runway during takeoff."

    B. I was embarrassed when Mrs. White said, "Your slip is showing!"

    C. "The middle school readers were unprepared to understand Bryant's poem 'Thanatopsis.'"

    D. The hall monitor yelled, "Fire! Fire!"

Answer: B. I was embarrassed when Mrs. White said, "Your slip is showing!"

Choice B is incorrectly punctuated because in sentences that are exclamatory, the exclamation point should be positioned outside the closing quotation marks if the quote itself is a statement, command, or cited title. The exclamation point is correctly positioned in choice D because the sentence is declarative, but the quotation is an exclamation.

(Average) (Skill 1.2)

16. Students who are learning English as a second language often require which of the following to process new information?

    A. Translators
    B. Reading tutors
    C. Instruction in their native language
    D. Additional time and repetitions

Answer: D. Additional time and repetitions

While there are varying thoughts and theories regarding the most appropriate instruction for ESL students, much ground can be gained by simply providing additional repetitions and time to gain understanding of new concepts. It is important to include visuals and activities using the other senses in every aspect of this instruction.

(Rigorous) (Skill 1.3)

17. A student who has difficulty pronouncing certain words or sounds may be demonstrating which speech and language disorder?

    A. Apraxia
    B. Articulation disorder
    C. Auditory processing
    D. Dysarthria

Answer: B. Articulation disorder

When children have difficulty pronouncing specific sounds, they may have an articulation disorder. It is important to remember that, with young children in particular, certain sounds are not expected to develop until

(Rigorous) (Skill 4.7)

18. Identify the type of appeal used by Molly Ivins's in this excerpt from her essay "Get a Knife, Get a Dog, But Get Rid of Guns."

    > As a civil libertarian, I, of course, support the Second Amendment. And I believe it means exactly what it says:

    > "A well regulated militia being necessary to the security of a free state, the right of the people to keep and bear arms shall not be infringed."

    A. Appeal based on writer's credibility
    B. Appeal to logic
    C. Appeal to the emotion
    D. Appeal to the reader

Answer: A. Appeal based on writer's credibility

By announcing that she is a civil libertarian and that she supports the Second Amendment, the author is establishing her credibility. At this point, Ivins has not provided reasons or appealed to the emotion, nor has she addressed the reader.

(Average) (Skill 7.9)

19. **"What is the point?" is the first question to be asked when:**
    A. Reading a written piece
    B. Listening to a presentation
    C. Writing a composition
    D. All of the above

    Answer: D. All of the above

    When reading, listening, or writing one should first ask, "What is the point?" The answer will be in the thesis. If a piece doesn't make a point, the reader/listener/viewer is likely to be confused or feel that it was not worth the effort.

(Easy) (Skill 10.4)

20. **All of the following are true about writing an introduction EXCEPT:**
    A. It should be written last
    B. It should lead the audience into the discourse
    C. It is the point of the paper
    D. It can take up a large percentage of the total word count

    Answer: C. It is the point of the paper

    The thesis is the point of the paper not the introduction. The rest of the choices are true about an introduction.

(Easy) (Skill 1.6)

21. **Children typically learn the majority of their words and phrases from:**
    A. School
    B. Reading
    C. Peers
    D. Other

    Answer: B. Reading

    Reading builds vocabulary, but in young children oral language develops from their environment.

(Average) (Skill 9.1)

22. **Isaac is mimicking the way his father is writing. He places a piece of paper on the table and holds the pencil in his hand correctly, but he merely draws lines and makes random marks on the paper. What type of writer is he?**
    A. Role play writer
    B. Emergent writer
    C. Developing writer
    D. Beginning writer

    Answer: A. Role play writer

    A role play writer uses writing-like behavior but has no phonetic association. He is aware of print but scribbles at this point.

(Easy) (Skill 3.3)

23. The basic features of the alphabetic principle include:

    A. Students need to be able to take spoken words apart and blend different sounds together to make new words.

    B. Students need to apply letter sounds to all their reading.

    C. The teaching of the alphabetic principle usually begins in kindergarten.

    D. All of the above

Answer: D. All of the above

All the stated answers above are features of the alphabetic principle. Another one not mentioned in the list above is that teachers need to use a systematic, effective program in order to teach children to read.

(Average) (Skill 10.3)

24. Topic sentences, transition words, and appropriate vocabulary are used by writers to:

    A. Meet various purposes

    B. Organize a multi-paragraph essay

    C. Express an attitude on a subject

    D. Explain the presentation of ideas

Answer: B. Organize a multi-paragraph essay

Correctly organizing an essay allows a writer to clearly communicate their ideas. To organize, a writer needs topic sentences, transition words, and appropriate vocabulary. Meeting a purpose, expressing an attitude, and explaining ideas are all done by an author in a piece of writing, but they are separate elements.

(Rigorous) (Skill 10.7)

25. Which of the following should students use to improve coherence of ideas within an argument?

    A. Transitional words or phrases to show relationship of ideas

    B. Conjunctions like "and" to join ideas together

    C. Use direct quotes extensively to improve credibility

    D. Adjectives and adverbs to provide stronger detail

Answer: A. Transitional words or phrases to show relationship of ideas

Transitional words and phrases are two-way indicators that connect the previous idea to the following idea. Sophisticated writers use transitional devices to clarify text (for example), to show contrast (despite), to show sequence (first, next), to show cause (because).

(Rigorous) (Skill 12.11)

26. When giving instructions, all of the following are important stylistic elements EXCEPT:

    A. Present in a serious and friendly tone

    B. Speak clearly and slowly

    C. Note the mood of the audience

    D. Review points of confusion

Answer: A. Present in a serious and friendly tone

Not all types of public speaking will have the same type of speaking style. When giving instructions, it is important to speak clearly and slowly, note the mood of the audience, and review if there is confusion. Presenting in a serious and friendly tone won't help the instructions be any more clear and is an important stylistic element of giving an oral presentation.

(Rigorous) (Skill 1.8)

27. **When speaking on a formal platform, students should do all of the following EXCEPT:**

    A. Use no contractions

    B. Have longer sentences

    C. Connect with the audience

    D. Strictly organize longer segments

    Answer: C. Connect with the audience

    When speaking formally, students should use fewer or no contractions, have longer sentences, and be more organized during longer segments of the speech. While connecting with the audience may seem beneficial, the personal antidotes or humorous pieces required to do that are not appropriate in a formal setting.

(Average) (Skill 1.9)

28. **To determine an author's purpose a reader must:**

    A. Use his or her own judgment.

    B. Verify all the facts.

    C. Link the causes to the effects.

    D. Rely on common sense.

    Answer: A. Use his or her own judgment.

An author may have more than one purpose in writing. There are no tricks or rules to follow, and the reader must use his or her own judgment to determine the author's purpose for writing. Verifying all the facts, linking causes to effects, and relying on common sense can all help a reader in judging the author's purpose, but none are solely responsible.

(Rigorous) (Skill 3.1)

29. **Julia has been hired to work in a school that serves a local public housing project. She is working with kindergarten children and has been asked to focus on shared reading. She selects:**

    A. Chapter books

    B. Riddle books

    C. Alphabet books

    D. Wordless picture books

    Answer: D. Wordless picture books

    Wordless picture books allow students to derive the story events from the illustrations and prevent stumbling over words they are unable to identify.

(Rigorous) (Skill 3.5)

30. **Four of Ms. Wolmark's students have lived in other countries. She is particularly pleased to be studying Sumerian proverbs with them as part of the fifth grade unit in analyzing the sayings of other cultures because:**

    A. This gives her a break from teaching, and the children can share sayings from other cultures they and their families have experienced

    B. This validates the experiences and expertise of ELL learners in her classroom

    C. This provides her children from the U.S. with a lens on other cultural values

    D. All of the above

    Answer: D. All of the above

    It is recommended that all teachers of reading and particularly those who are working with ELL students use meaningful, student centered, and culturally customized activities. These activities may include: language games, word walls, and poems. Some of these activities might, if possible, be initiated in the child's first language and then reiterated in English.

(Average) (Skill 7.2)

31. **Which of the following is an important feature of vocabulary instruction, according to the National Reading Panel?**

    A. Repetition of vocabulary items

    B. Keeping a consistent task structure at all times

    C. Teaching vocabulary in more than one language

    D. Isolating vocabulary instruction from other subjects

    Answer: A. Repetition of vocabulary items

    According to the National Reading Panel, repetition and multiple exposures to vocabulary items are important. Students should be given items that will be likely to appear in many contexts.

(Rigorous) (Skill 10.6)

32. **Exposition occurs within a story:**

    A. After the rising action

    B. After the denouement

    C. Before the rising action

    D. Before the setting

    Answer: C. Before the rising action

    Exposition is where characters and their situations are introduced. *Rising action* is the point at which conflict starts to occur and is often a turning point. *Denouement* is the final resolution of the plot.

(Easy) (Skill 1.5)

33. **The idea that students need to be able to take spoken words apart and blend different sounds together to make words describes:**

    A. The alphabetic principle

    B. Syntax

    C. Phonics

    D. Morphology

    Answer: A. The alphabetic principle

The alphabet principle consists of four basic features. The first feature is listed in the question above; the other three are discussed here. These principles are:

- Students need to apply letter sounds to all their reading.
- Teachers need to use a systematic, effective program in order to teach children to read.
- The teaching of the alphabetic principle usually begins in kindergarten.

(Easy) (Skill 3.2)

34. Which of the following strategies encourages print awareness in classrooms?

    A. Word walls
    B. Using big books to read to students
    C. Using highlighters to locate uppercase letters
    D. All of the above

Answer: D. All of the above

Classrooms rich in print provide many opportunities for students to see, use, and experience text in various forms. Word walls, big books, and highlighting certain textual features are all ways to expose students to various forms of text.

(Easy) (Skill 4.5)

35. Teaching students how to interpret _____ involves evaluating a text's headings, subheadings, bolded words, and side notes.

    A. graphic organizers
    B. text structure
    C. textual marking
    D. summaries

Answer: B. Text structures

Studying text structures, including the table of contents, glossary, index, headings, etc., is an excellent way for students to increase comprehension of a text. Knowledge of these tools helps students to understand the organization and flow of their reading.

(Average) (Skill 6.3)

36. The complex linguistic deficiency marked by the inability to remember and recognize words by sounds and, further, the inability to break words down into component units describes:

    A. Oral processing disorder
    B. Attention deficit disorder
    C. Dyslexia
    D. None of the above

Answer: C. Dyslexia

Dyslexia is a very common reading disorder term used to describe most severe difficulties in learning to read and/or write. It is a very complex linguistic deficiency that typically displays problems recalling or recognizing words, as well as the inability to decode words. Oral processing disorder concerns a student's ability to listen to and process audible information, while attention deficit disorder concerns a student's ability to focus and maintain attention.

(Rigorous) (Skill 6.4)

37. **Academically, appropriate literature primarily helps students to _____.**

    A. become better readers

    B. see how the skills they learned are applied to writing

    C. enjoy library time

    D. increase academic skills in other content areas

Answer: B. see how the skills they learned are applied to writing

When students are exposed to appropriate literature selections, and are taught to select appropriate texts for themselves, they are able to observe how the reading and writing skills they learn in classroom mini-lessons are applied to published writing. Published works are an excellent place for students to see not only proper conventions of grammar, but "real-life" examples of imagery and figurative language.

(Average) (Skill 9.3)

38. **Which of the following is NOT an effective strategy to aid students with spelling instruction?**

    A. Knowledge of patterns, sounds, and letter-sound association

    B. Memorizing sight words

    C. Writing words one or two times

    D. Writing the words correctly in personal writing

Answer: C. Writing words one or two times

Answers A, B and D are all effective strategies listed within the content of this book to aid students with spelling instruction. Writing words multiple times, rather than just once or twice, is another effective strategy.

(Rigorous) (Skill 9.1)

39. **Which number order below displays the appropriate sequence for developing writing skills?**

    1. Experimental writing
    2. Early writing
    3. Role-play writing
    4. Conventional writing

    A. 1, 4, 2, 3

    B. 3, 1, 2, 4

    C. 3, 2, 1, 4

    D. 1, 2, 4, 3

Answer: B. 3, 1, 2, 4

The correct order for the stages of writing development are role-play writing, experimental writing, early writing, and finally, conventional writing.

(Rigorous) (Skill 9.3)

40. **In the _____ stage of writing, students write in scribbles and can assign meaning to the markings.**

    A. role-play writing

    B. experimental writing

    C. early writing

    D. conventional writing

Answer: A. role-play writing

In the role-playing stage, the child writes in scribbles and assigns a message to the symbols. Even though an adult would not be able to read the writing, the child can read what is written, although it may not be the same each time the child reads it. In experimental writing, the student writes in the simplest form of recognizable writing. In the early writing stage, children start to use a small range of familiar text forms and sight words in their writing. Finally, in the conventional writing stage, students have a sense of audience and purpose for writing.

MATH

(Average) (Skill 14.1)

41. Which of the following statements best characterizes the meaning of "absolute value of x"?

   A. The square root of x

   B. The square of x

   C. The distance on a number line between x and $-x$

   D. The distance on a number line between 0 and x

Answer: D. The distance on a number line between 0 and x

The absolute value of a number x is best described as the distance on a number line between 0 and x, regardless of whether x is positive or negative. Note that the following expression is valid for $x \geq 0$: $|x| = |-x|$

(Average) (Skill 14.2)

42. Which number is equivalent to the following expression?

   $3 \times 10^3 + 9 \times 10^0 + 6 + 10^{-2} + 8 \times 10^{-3}$

   A. 3,900.68

   B. 3,009.068

   C. 39.68

   D. 309.068

Answer: B. 3,009.068

Each product represents a digit in a specific place in the decimal. We can find the value of the number by calculating the products and adding, or by simply noting that the 3 is in the thousands place, the 9 is in the ones place, the 6 is in the hundredths place, and the 8 is in the thousandths place. Zeroes are in all other places.

$3 \times 10^3 + 9 \times 10^0 + 6 + 10^{-2} + 8 \times 10^{-3} = 3{,}0009.068$

(Average) (Skill 14.5)

43. Which of the following terms most accurately describes the set of numbers below?

   $\{3, \sqrt{16}, \pi^0, 6, \frac{28}{4}\}$

   A. Rationals

   B. Irrationals

   C. Complex

   D. Whole numbers

Answer: D. Whole numbers

Let's simplify the set of numbers as follows.

{3, 4, 1, 6, 7}

Note that this set of numbers can be described as real numbers, rationals, integers, and whole numbers, but they are best described as whole numbers.

(Average) (Skill 14.7)

44. **Calculate the value of the following expression.**

    $\left(\frac{6}{3} + 1 \cdot 5\right)^2 \cdot \frac{1}{7} + (3 \cdot 2 - 1)$

    A. 6
    B. 10
    C. 12
    D. 294

    Answer: C. 12

    Apply the correct order of operations to get the correct result: first, calculate all terms in parentheses, followed by exponents, division and multiplication, and addition and subtraction (in that order).

    $(2 + 5)^2 \cdot \left(\frac{1}{7}\right) + (6 - 1) = 7^2 \cdot \frac{1}{7} + 5 = 49 \cdot \frac{1}{7} + 5 = 7 + 5 = 12$

(Rigorous) (Skill 14.8)

45. **What is the GCF of 12, 30, 56, and 144?**

    A. 2
    B. 3
    C. 5
    D. 7

    Answer: A. 2

One way to determine the greatest common factor (GCF) is to list the factors for each number. Although this can be tedious, it is a relatively sure method of determining the GCF. Note that you need not determine any factors larger than the smallest number in the list (12, in this case)—12 doesn't have any factors greater than 12.

12: 2, 3, 4, 6, 12
30: 2, 3, 5, 6, 10
56: 2, 4, 7, 8
144: 2, 3, 4, 6, 8, 9, 12

By inspection of these lists, we see that 2 is the greatest common factor.

(Rigorous) (Skill 13.9)

46. **In a certain classroom, 32% of the students are male. What is the minimum number of females in the class?**

    A. 68
    B. 34
    C. 32
    D. 17

    Answer: D. 17

    Obviously, the classroom can only have a whole number of students. Let's call this number x. We know that $0.32x$ is the number of males; the number of females must then be $0.68x$. If f is the number of females, then

    $f = \frac{68}{100}x$

    Since f is a whole number, we must find the smallest value of x for which $68x$ is divisible by 100. But if we simplify the fraction, then

    $f = \frac{17}{25}x$

Thus, we see that $x = 25$ is a possibility. Because 17 is a prime number and x must be a whole number, $x = 25$ is the smallest possible value. Then,

$f = \frac{17}{25}(25) = 17$

The classroom must therefore have a minimum of 17 female students.

(Average) (Skill 13.2)

47. The final cost of an item (with sales tax) is $8.35. If the sales tax is 7%, what was the pre-tax price of the item?

    A. $7.80
    B. $8.00
    C. $8.28
    D. $8.93

Answer: A. $7.80

We can solve this problem by constructing a proportionality expression. Let's call the pre-tax price of the item x; then, if we add 7% of x to this price, we get a final cost of $8.35.

$x + 0.07x = \$8.35$
$1.07x = \$8.35$
$x = \frac{\$8.35}{1.07} = \$7.80$

Thus, the initial price of the item was $7.80 (answer A). You can also determine this answer by multiplying each option by 1.07; the correct answer is the one that yields a product of $8.35.

(Average) (Skill 16.9)

48. A traveler uses a ruler and finds the distance between two cities to be 3.5 inches. If the legend indicates that 100 miles is the same as an inch, what is the distance in miles between the cities?

    A. 29 miles
    B. 35 miles
    C. 100 miles
    D. 350 miles

Answer: D. 350 miles

Construct a proportion relating inches to miles. Let the unknown distance in miles be d.

$\frac{100 \text{ miles}}{1 \text{ inch}} = \frac{d}{3.5 \text{ inches}}$

Cross multiply to find the value of d.

$d = 3.5 \text{ inches} \frac{100 \text{ miles}}{1 \text{ inch}} = 350 \text{ miles}$

(Average) (Skill 15.7)

49. A burning candle loses $\frac{1}{2}$ inch in height every hour. If the original height of the candle was 6 inches, which of the following equations describes the relationship between the height h of the candle and the number of hours t since it was lit?

    A. $2h + t = 12$
    B. $2h - t = 12$
    C. $h = 6 - t$
    D. $h = 0.5t + 6$

Answer: A. $2h + t = 12$

Since the height of the candle is falling, the slope $= -\frac{1}{2}$. Thus, the equation in the slope-intercept form is $h = -\left(\frac{1}{2}\right)t + 6$ since $h = 6$ for $t = 0$. Multiplying both sides of the equation by 2, we get $2h = -t + 12$ or $2h + t = 12$.

(Average) (Skill 15.1)

50. Three less than four times a number is five times the sum of that number and 6. Which equation could be used to solve this problem?

    A. $3 - 4n = 5(n + 6)$
    B. $3 - 4n + 5n = 6$
    C. $4n - 3 = 5n + 6$
    D. $4n - 3 = 5(n + 6)$

    Answer: D. $4n - 3 = 5(n + 6)$

    Be sure to enclose the sum of the number and 6 in parentheses.

(Rigorous) (Skill 15.4)

51. Which set is closed under addition?

    A. $\{0, \frac{1}{2}, \frac{1}{4}, \frac{1}{8}, \frac{1}{16}, \ldots\}$
    B. $\{\ldots, -2, -1, 0, 1, 2, \ldots\}$
    C. $\{-1, 0, 1\}$
    D. $\{0, 1, 2, 3, 4, 5\}$

    Answer: B. $\{\ldots, -2, -1, 0, 1, 2, \ldots\}$

    For a set to be closed under a particular operation, then that operation performed on any two members of the set must yield a result that is also a member of the set. Thus, we can easily show that choices A, C, and D are not closed under addition by counterexamples. For answer A, $\frac{1}{2} + \frac{1}{2} = 1$, but 1 is not a member of the set. Likewise, for answer C, $1 + 1 = 2$, but 2 is not a member of the set. The same type of reasoning can be applied to choice D. For choice B (the set of integers), however, we know that the sum of any two integers is another integer. Thus, the set of numbers in B is closed under addition.

(Average) (Skill 15.2)

52. Which property justifies the following manipulation?

    $x^2 - 3y \rightarrow 3y + x^2$

    A. Associative
    B. Commutative
    C. Distributive
    D. None of the above

    Answer: B. Commutative

    The commutative property tells us that $a + b = b + a$; thus, the manipulation of the algebraic expression in the problem statement can be justified by the commutative property.

(Rigorous) (Skill 15.6)

53. Which set cannot be considered "dense"?

    A. Integers
    B. Rationals
    C. Irrationals
    D. Reals

    Answer: A. Integers

    A set of numbers is considered dense if between any two arbitrary values from the set, there exists another value from the set that lies between these two values. For instance, between 1 and 3 is the number 2. For integers, however, there is no integer between 1 and 2, for example (or between any two consecutive integers). Thus, the correct answer is choice A. For the other sets (rationals, irrationals, and reals), there is always a value between any two arbitrary values from those sets.

(Average) (Skill 15.3)

54. Which of the following is an example of a multiplicative inverse?

   A. $x^2 - x^2 = 0$
   B. $(y - 3)^0 = 1$
   C. $\frac{1}{e^{3z}} = 1$
   D. $f^2 = \frac{1}{g}$

   Answer: C. $\frac{1}{e^{3z}} = 1$

   A multiplicative inverse has the form:
   $a \cdot \frac{1}{a} = 1$

   Thus, answer C best fits this definition.

(Rigorous) (Skill 15.10)

55. Two farmers are buying feed for animals. One farmer buys eight bags of grain and six bales of hay for $105, and the other farmer buys three bags of grain and nine bales of hay for $69.75. How much is a bag of grain?

   A. $4.50
   B. $9.75
   C. $14.25
   D. $28.50

   Answer: B. $9.75

   Let x be the price of a bag of grain, and let y be the price of a bale of hay. We can then write two equations based on the information provided in the problem.

   Farmer 1: $8x + 6y = \$105$

   Farmer 2: $3x + 9y = \$69.75$

   We want to find x, the price of a bag of grain. One approach to solving this problem is to solve either the first or second equation for y and then substitute the result into the other equation and solve for x. Another approach involves subtraction. Let's multiply both sides of the second equation by $\frac{2}{3}$.

   $\frac{2}{3}(3x + 9y = \$69.75)$

   $2x + 6y = \$46.50$

   Now, subtract this from the first equation.

   $$\begin{array}{r} 8x + 6y = \$105 \\ - \ 2x + 6y = \$46.50 \\ \hline 6x = \$58.5 \end{array}$$

   Solving for x yields the solution.

   $x = \$9.75$

(Rigorous) (Skill 15.9)

56. Which expression best characterizes the shaded area in the graph below?

   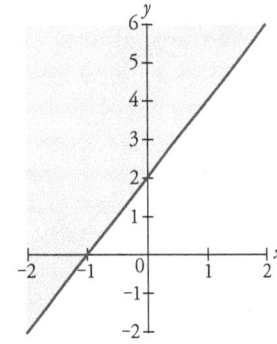

   A. $y \leq -x + 2$
   B. $y \geq 2x + 2$
   C. $y = 2x + 2$
   D. $y \geq 2x - 1$

   Answer: B. $y \geq 2x + 2$

   The shaded region includes all the points above the line. Thus, we need only find the equation for the line and then choose the correct symbol for the inequality. Note that the line has a slope of 2 (it increases by two units in the y direction for every one unit of increase in the *x* direction) and a *y*-intercept of 2. Thus, the equation for the line is

$y = 2x + 2$

Note that the shaded region is above the line; the best choice is then answer B, or $y \geq 2x + 2$.

(Rigorous) (Skill 15.5)

57. Solve for L:

    $R = r + \dfrac{400(W - L)}{N}$

    A. $L = W - \dfrac{N}{400}(R - r)$
    B. $L = W + \dfrac{N}{400}(R - r)$
    C. $L = W - \dfrac{400}{N}(R - r)$
    D. $L = \dfrac{NR}{r} = 400W$

    Answer: A. $L = W - \dfrac{N}{400}(R - r)$

    $R = r + \dfrac{400(W - L)}{N}$;
    $\Rightarrow R - r = \dfrac{400(W - L)}{N}$;
    $\Rightarrow \dfrac{N}{400}(R - r) = W - L$;
    $\Rightarrow L = W - \dfrac{N}{400}(R - r)$

(Rigorous) (Skill 16.2)

58. The formula for the volume of a cylinder is $V = \pi r^2 h$ where *r* is the radius of the cylinder and *h* is its height. What is the volume of a cylinder of diameter 2 cm and height 5 cm?

    A. 25π cm²
    B. 5π cm²
    C. 20π cm²
    D. 50π cm²

Answer: B. 5π cm²

Since the diameter of the cylinder is 2 cm, the radius is 1 cm. Hence,

$V = \pi r^2 h = \pi(1)^2(5) = 5\pi$ cm²

(Rigorous) (Skill 16.7)

59. The figure below is an equilateral triangle. Which transformation converts the solid-line figure to the broken-line figure?

A. Rotation
B. Reflection
C. Glide reflection
D. Any of the above

Answer: D. Any of the above

Because the triangle is equilateral, any of the geometric transformations listed above can be used to convert the solid-line triangle to the broken-line triangle. For a rotation, the center of rotation is chosen halfway between the two figures as shown below.

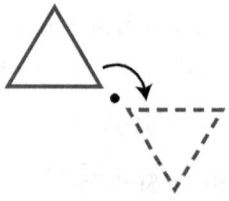

A reflection likewise requires a correctly chosen line of reflection, which acts like a mirror for the figure.

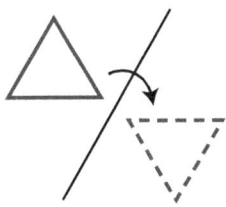

Finally, a glide reflection can also perform the transformation. A glide reflection is simply a translation followed by a reflection (or vice versa).

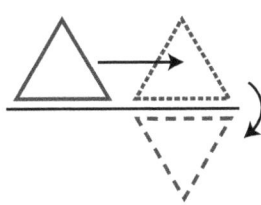

(Rigorous) (Skill 16.6)

60. **Which of the following is a net of a cube?**

    A.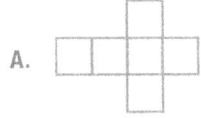

    B.

    C.

    D.

Answer: A.

A net is a two-dimensional figure that can be folded (along the interior line segments) to form a three-dimensional figure of a specific type. Answer A is the only figure that is a net of a cube.

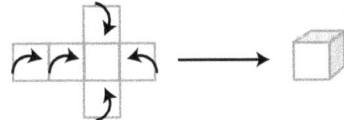

(Rigorous) (Skill 16.3)

61. **What is the length of the shortest side of a right isosceles triangle if the longest side is 5 centimeters?**

    A. 2.24 centimeters

    B. 2.5 centimeters

    C. 3.54 centimeters

    D. Not enough information

Answer: C. 3.54 centimeters

If a triangle is isosceles, then two of its sides are congruent, as are two of its angles. The longest side of such a triangle must be the hypotenuse; the other two sides, the legs, must be of equal length (this is because the congruent angles must be less than 90° each). Let's call the length of a leg x. Then, using the Pythagorean theorem,

$$x^2 + x^2 = 2x^2 = 5^2 = 25$$

$$x^2 = \frac{25}{2} = 12.5$$

$$x \sqrt{12.5} \approx 3.54$$

Thus, the shortest side (the legs are congruent) of the triangle described in the problem is 3.54 centimeters.

(Average) (Skill 16.4)

62. What is the area of the shaded region below, where the circle has a radius r?

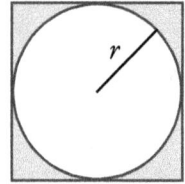

A. r^2

B. $(4 - \pi)r^2$

C. $(2 - \pi)r^2$

D. $4\pi r^2$

Answer: B. $(4 - \pi)r^2$

Notice that the figure is a circle of radius r inscribed in a quadrilateral—this quadrilateral must therefore be a square. Thus, the sides of the square each have a length twice that of the radius, as shown below.

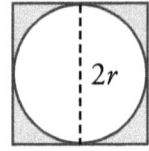 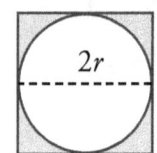

To find the area of the shaded region, subtract the area of the circle (πr^2) from the area of the square ($4r^2$).

$A_{shaded} = 4r^2 - \pi r^2 = (4 - \pi)r^2$

(Average) (Skill 16.8)

63. The figure below is constructed with congruent equilateral triangles each having sides of length 4 units. What is the perimeter of the figure?

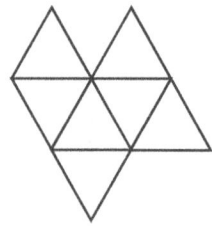

A. 9 units

B. 36 units

C. 60 units

D. Not enough information

Answer: B. 36 units

To determine the perimeter, simply count the number of external sides of the figure and multiply the result by 4 units (each side of each triangle, according to the problem, has a length of 4 units). The figure has nine sides, so the perimeter is 36 units.

(Average) (Skill 17.2)

64. The following stem and leaf plot shows rainfall data in inches over several consecutive days. What is the median value?

0	7
1	3 9
2	1 5 7 8
3	0 3 4 6 6 9
4	3 5 5 7 8
5	0 0 3 5
10	3

A. 3.6 in

B. 3.9 in

C. 4.3 in

D. 3.4 in

Answer: B. 3.9 in

Since there are 23 data points, the median or middle value is the 12th one.

(Rigorous) (Skill 17.4)

65. A bag contains four red marbles and six blue marbles. If three selections are made without replacement, what is the probability of choosing three red marbles?

   A. $\frac{3}{10}$

   B. $\frac{8}{125}$

   C. $\frac{1}{30}$

   D. $\frac{1}{60}$

Answer: C. $\frac{1}{30}$

Because the question tells us that this experiment is performed without replacement, we know that each time a marble is chosen, it is not returned to the bag. In the first selection, the probability of choosing a red marble is 4 out of 10, or $\frac{2}{5}$. In this case, a red marble is removed from the bag leaving three red marbles and six blue marbles. The probability of then making another selection of a red marble is three out of nine, or $\frac{1}{3}$. This leaves two red marbles and six blue marbles. The probability of selecting a red marble in the final selection is then two out of eight, or $\frac{1}{4}$. To determine the probability of these three selections occurring consecutively, we multiply the probabilities from each step.

$P(\text{three red}) = \frac{2}{5} \cdot \frac{1}{3} \cdot \frac{1}{4} = \frac{2}{60} = \frac{1}{30}$

Thus, we have a $\frac{1}{30}$ chance of selecting (without replacement) three red marbles consecutively.

(Average) (Skill 17.3)

66. What is the sample space for the sum of the outcomes for two rolls of a six-sided die?

   A. {1, 2, 3, 4, 5, 6}

   B. {1, 2, 3, 4, 5, 6, 7, 8, 9, 10, 11, 12}

   C. {2, 3, 4, 5, 6, 7, 8, 9, 10, 11, 12}

   D. {7, 8, 9, 10, 11, 12}

Answer: C. {2, 3, 4, 5, 6, 7, 8, 9, 10, 11, 12}

A six-sided die can turn up any number between one and six, inclusive. The smallest sum that could be obtained from two rolls is for the case where both rolls turn up a one—the sum would then be two. The maximum sum would be the case where both rolls turn up a six—the sum would then be 12. Thus, the sample space for this experiment is 2 through 12, inclusive.

(Rigorous) (Skill 17.5)

67. How many different three-card hands can be drawn from a standard deck of 52 playing cards?

   A. 156

   B. 2,704

   C. 132,600

   D. 140,608

Answer: C. 132,600

Each card in the deck is unique. To determine how many different three-card hands we could get, we need to multiply the number of possibilities for each card selection. In the first selection, we have 52 possible choices. In the second, we have 51 choices, and in the third, we have 50 choices. The number of possible hands, n, is the product of these three numbers.

$$n = 52 \cdot 51 \cdot 50 = 132{,}600$$

(Rigorous) (Skill 14.5)

68. The number "0" is a member of all of the following groups of numbers EXCEPT:

    A. Whole numbers
    B. Real numbers
    C. Natural numbers
    D. Integers

Answer: C. Natural numbers

The number zero is a whole number, real number, and an integer, but the natural numbers (also known as the counting numbers) start with the number one, not zero.

(Rigorous) (Skill 13.8)

69. Students in Mr. Anderson's class want to know which train car will hold more plastic apples: the long, thin car, or the square car. First, they fill the long, thin car with apples and record their answer. Then they fill the square car with apples and record their answer. Which math principles does this activity demonstrate?

    A. Problem solving, subtraction
    B. Subtraction, meaningful counting
    C. Problem solving, number sense
    D. Addition, problem solving

Answer: C. Problem solving, number sense

The students are using problem solving skills by experimenting to see which train car can hold more plastic apples. They demonstrate number sense as they count both sets of apples to determine which set has more.

(Easy) (Skill 16.4)

70. In a _____ all sides are the same length and all angles are the same measure.

    A. triangle
    B. regular polygon
    C. sphere
    D. parallelogram

Answer: B. regular polygon

In a regular polygon all sides are the same length and all angles are the same measure. A triangle is a polygon, but the sides are not always the same length. A sphere is a three-dimensional symmetrical figure. Finally, a parallelogram is a quadrilateral figure with two sets of parallel sides; however, all four sides are not the same length.

(Easy) (Skill 16.7)

71. Which letter does not demonstrate symmetry?

    A. T
    B. A
    C. O
    D. F

    Answer: D. F

    If printed on a piece of paper, each of the other letters could be folded in half, and each half would be identical.

(Rigorous) (Skill 18.9)

72. Which types of graphs would best be used to represent the number of students who like red, green, or yellow best?

    A. A bar graph or pictograph
    B. A pictograph or line graph
    C. A stem and leaf plot or bar graph
    D. A line graph or stem and leaf plot

    Answer: A. A bar graph or pictograph

    A line graph is the most effective way to show change over time. Bar graphs and pictographs show quantity, or sometimes the results of a survey—in this case, the color that each student likes best. Stem and leaf plots show lists of numbers, such as test scores, in a specialized format.

(Rigorous) (Skill 18.1)

73. Students in a kindergarten class are curious about which toy is heavier: a plastic doll or a metal truck. They use a balance and wooden cubes to determine their answer. The toy that requires more cubes to hold the balance even will be the heavier toy. Which math principles does this activity demonstrate?

    A. Subtraction, meaningful counting
    B. Problem solving, number sense
    C. Addition, problem solving
    D. Problem solving, subtraction

    Answer: B. Problem solving, number sense

    In this activity, students are using math problem solving through experimentation. Because of their number sense, they are able to determine which toy is heavier (weighs the same as more blocks).

SOCIAL SCIENCES

(Average) (Skill 21.2)

74. Denver is called the "mile-high city" because it is:

    A. Located approximately one mile above the plains of eastern Colorado
    B. Located exactly one mile above the base of Cheyenne Mountain
    C. Located approximately one mile above sea level
    D. The city with the tallest buildings in Colorado

    Answer: C. Located approximately one mile above sea level

Elevations of cities are calculated according to the height above sea level. That fact negates all answers except C.

(Rigorous) (Skill 21.3)

75. The state of Louisiana is divided into parishes. What type of region do the parishes represent?

    A. Formal region
    B. Functional region
    C. Vernacular region
    D. Human region

Answer: A. Formal region

There are three main types of regions. Formal regions are areas defined by actual political boundaries, such as a city, county, or state. Functional regions are defined by a common function, such as the area covered by a telephone service. Vernacular regions are less formally defined areas that are formed by people's perception (e.g., "the Middle East" or "the South").

(Average) (Skill 21.1)

76. Which continent is only one country?

    A. Australia
    B. New Zealand
    C. The Arctic
    D. Antarctica

Answer: A. Australia

Of the seven continents, Australia is the only one that contains just one country. It is also the only island continent. Antarctica is the southernmost continent. It surrounds the South Pole. New Zealand is made up of two large islands, but it is not a continent. The Arctic is a region that includes parts of several continents, but is not in and of itself a continent. In fact, much of the Arctic is ice-covered ocean.

(Rigorous) (Skill 19.10)

77. The Southern Hemisphere contains all of which continent?

    A. Africa
    B. Australia
    C. South America
    D. North America

Answer: B. Australia

The Southern Hemisphere, located between the South Pole and the Equator, contains all of Australia, a small part of Asia, about one-third of Africa, most of South America, and all of Antarctica.

(Average) (Skill 20.2)

78. Anthropology is:

    A. The profession that made the Leakey family famous
    B. The scientific study of human culture and humanity
    C. Not related to geography at all
    D. Margaret Mead's study of the Samoans

Answer: B. The scientific study of human culture and humanity

Anthropology did make the Leakeys famous (choice A) but that does not define anthropology. The text states that anthropology is related to geography (choice C). Margaret Mead's study of the Samoans (choice D) is only one part of anthropology.

(Rigorous) (Skill 21.8)

79. In the 1920s, Margaret Mead wrote *Coming of Age in Samoa,* relating her observations about this group's way of life. What of these types of geographical study best describes her method?

    A. Regional
    B. Topical
    C. Physical
    D. Human

Answer: D. Human

Mead studied the Samoans' human activity patterns and how they related to the environment including political, cultural, historical, urban, and social geographical fields of study. Regional study is limited to the elements and characteristics of a place or region. In a topical, a research would focus on an earth feature or one human activity occurring throughout the entire world. In a physical study, the researcher would focus on the earth's physical features and what creates and changes them, how they relate to each other and to human activities.

(Rigorous) (Skill 21.26)

80. Which activity is most likely to have a negative environmental impact on an area?

    I. Building a new skyscraper in Manhattan
    II. Strip mining for coal in West Virginia
    III. Digging a new oil well within an existing oilfield in Texas
    IV. Building ten new homes in a 100-acre suburban neighborhood that already contains fifty homes

    A. II and III only
    B. II only
    C. I only
    D. I and IV only

Answer: B. II only

Strip mining sometimes involves using dynamite to remove the top of a mountain and is thus very harmful to an environment. In regard to oil wells and skyscrapers; building one new oil well in an existing oilfield or one new skyscraper in Manhattan (which already has a high concentration of skyscrapers) won't make an extremely heavy environmental impact. Building the ten new homes in an existing neighborhood where there is plenty of room for expansion will probably have only a modest environmental impact.

(Average) (Skill 22.2)

81. Which of the following are two agricultural innovations that began in China?

    A. Using pesticides and fertilizer

    B. Irrigation and cuneiform

    C. Improving the silk industry and inventing gunpowder

    D. Terrace farming and crop rotation

Answer: D. Terrace farming and crop rotation

Pesticides and fertilizer (choice A) are modern innovations. It was the Sumerians who introduced irrigation and cuneiform (choice B), not the Chinese. The Chinese did improve the silk industry and invent gunpowder (choice C), but these are not agricultural innovations.

(Average) (Skill 21.21)

82. Which civilization laid the foundations of geometry?

    A. Egyptian

    B. Greek

    C. Roman

    D. Chinese

Answer: B. Greek

In the field of mathematics, Pythagoras and Euclid laid the foundation of geometry and Archimedes calculated the value of *pi* during the Ancient Greek civilization. Egypt made numerous significant contributions, including the invention of the method of counting in groups of 1–10 (the decimal system). The contributions and accomplishments of the Romans are numerous, but their greatest included language, engineering, building, law, government, roads, trade, and the "Pax Romana," the long period of peace enabling free travel and trade, spreading people, cultures, goods, and ideas all over a vast area of the known world. The Chinese studied nature and weather; stressed the importance of education, family, and a strong central government; followed the religions of Buddhism, Confucianism, and Taoism; and invented such things as gunpowder, paper, printing, and the magnetic compass.

(Average) (Skill 20.8)

83. The international organization established to work for world peace at the end of the Second World War is the:

    A. League of Nations

    B. United Federation of Nations

    C. United Nations

    D. United World League

Answer: C. United Nations

The international organization established to work for world peace at the end of the Second World War was the United Nations. From the ashes of the failed League of Nations, established following World War I, the United Nations continues to be a major player in world affairs today.

(Rigorous) (Skill 23.10)

84. In December, Ms. Griffin asks her students to talk about their holiday traditions. Rebecca explains about lighting the nine candles during Chanukkah, Josh explains about the lighting of the seven candles during Kwanzaa, and Bernard explains about lighting the

four candles during Advent. This is an example of:

A. Cultural diffusion

B. Cultural identity

C. Cross-cultural exchanges

D. Cosmopolitanism

Answer: C. Cross-cultural exchanges

Cross-cultural exchanges involved the discovery of shared values and needs as well as an appreciation of differences. Cultural diffusion is the movement of cultural ideas or materials between populations independent of the movement of those populations. Cultural identity is the identification of individuals or groups as they are influenced by their belonging to a particular group or culture. Cosmopolitanism blurs cultural differences in the creation of a shared new culture.

(Average) (Skill 21.10)

85. **English and Spanish colonists took what from Native Americans?**

    A. Land

    B. Water rights

    C. Money

    D. Religious beliefs

Answer: A. Land

The settlers took a lot of land from the Native Americans. Water rights (choice B), money (choice C), and religious beliefs (choice D) are not mentioned as areas of contention between the European settlers and the Native Americans.

(Average) (Skill 20.4)

86. **Spanish colonies were:**

    A. Mainly in the northeast

    B. Mainly in the south

    C. Mainly in the Midwest

    D. Mainly in Canada

Answer: B. Mainly in the south

English colonies were in the northeast (choice A). What is now the Midwest (choice C) had not yet been settled by Europeans. French colonies were in "the extreme north," which is present-day Canada (choice D).

(Rigorous) (Skill 20.18)

87. **In the events leading up to the American Revolution, which of these methods was effective in dealing with the British taxes?**

    A. Boycotts

    B. Strikes

    C. Armed conflicts

    D. Resolutions

Answer: A. Boycotts

In several instances, boycotts were effective in convincing the British to repeat taxes. For example in 1765, merchants boycotted imported English goods, and the Stamp Act was repealed three months later. In 1767, boycotts led to the repeal of the Townshend Acts. Strikes were not a factor. Armed conflicts tended to strengthen British resolve and resolutions had no weight. Boycotts affected the British economy and achieved greater success for the colonies.

(Rigorous) (Skill 20.16)

88. **One of the political parties that developed in the early 1790s was led by:**

    A. Thomas Jefferson
    B. George Washington
    C. Aaron Burr
    D. John Quincy Adams

    Answer: A. Thomas Jefferson

    George Washington (choice B) "warned against the creation of 'factions.'" Aaron Burr (choice C) is the man who killed Alexander Hamilton in a duel. John Quincy Adams (choice D) was not active in politics until the 1820s.

(Easy) (Skill 20.20)

89. **How did the labor force change after 1830?**

    A. Employers began using children
    B. Employers began hiring immigrants
    C. Employers began hiring women
    D. Employers began hiring non-immigrant men

    Answer: B. Employers began hiring immigrants

    Employers began hiring immigrants who were arriving in large numbers. Children (choice A) and women (choice C) began entering the labor force prior to 1830. Employers had always used non-immigrant men (choice D).

(Rigorous) (Skill 20.22)

90. **Which of these was not a result of World War I in the United States?**

    A. Establishment of new labor laws
    B. Prosperous industrial growth
    C. Formation of the United Nations
    D. Growth of the stock market

    Answer: C. Formation of the United Nations

    The United Nations was formed after World War II. After World War I, the League of Nations formed and established the United States in a central position in international relations that would increase in importance through the century.

(Average) (Skill 23.1)

91. **Among civilized people:**

    A. Strong government is not necessary
    B. Systems of control are rudimentary at best
    C. Government has no sympathy for individuals or for individual happiness
    D. Governments began to assume more institutional forms

    Answer: D. Governments began to assume more institutional forms

    Absence of strong government (choice A) is harmful. Systems of government that are rudimentary at best (choice B) are not suitable for civilized people. It is not true that government among civilized people has no sympathy for individuals or for individual happiness (choice C).

(Rigorous) (Skill 23.2)

92. The U.S. House of Representatives has:

   A. 100 members

   B. 435 members

   C. Three branches

   D. A president and a vice president

Answer: B. 435 members

The U.S. Senate has 100 members (choice A). The U.S. government as a whole has three branches (choice C). The executive branch of the U.S. government has a president and a vice-president (choice D).

(Rigorous) (Skill 23.5)

93. Socialism is:

   A. A system of government with a legislature

   B. A system where the government is subject to a vote of "no confidence"

   C. A political belief and system in which the state takes a guiding role in the national economy

   D. A system of government with three distinct branches

Answer: C. A political belief and system in which the state takes a guiding role in the national economy

Socialism does not involve a legislature (choice A). A vote of "no confidence" (choice B) is associated with a parliamentary system, not with socialism. The U.S. government has three branches (choice D). This is not socialism.

(Average) (Skill 23.3)

94. Which of the following was not a source of conflict in writing the U.S. Constitution?

   A. Establishing a monarchy

   B. Equalizing power between the small states and the large states

   C. Dealing with slavery

   D. Electing a president

Answer: A. Establishing a monarchy

Although the British system of government was the basis of the U.S. Constitution, the delegates to the Constitutional Convention were divided on the way power would be held. Some wanted a strong, centralized, individual authority. Others feared autocracy or the growth of monarchy. The compromise was to give the president broad powers but to limit the amount of time, through term of office, that any individual could exercise that power.

(Rigorous) (Skill 23.8)

95. Upon arrest, a person is read a "Miranda warning" which reads, in part, "You have the right to remain silent. Anything you say can and will be used against you in a court of law." Under what amendment in the Bill of Rights is this covered?

   A. The right against unreasonable search and seizures

   B. The right to trial by jury and right to legal council

   C. The right against self-incrimination

   D. The right to jury trial for civil actions

Answer: C. The right against self-incrimination

According to the Fifth Amendment, a citizen has the privilege to prevent self-incrimination. Law enforcement officials advise a suspect in custody of his/her right to remain silent. While the right to council is also part of the Miranda warning, it is not part of the question as written here.

(Rigorous) (Skill 22.5)

96. **The equilibrium price:**
    A. Is the price that clears the markets
    B. Is the price in the middle
    C. Identifies a shortage or a surplus
    D. Is an agricultural price support

Answer: A. Is the price that clears the markets

The price in the middle (choice B) is related to the principle of equilibrium, but it is not the equilibrium price. The equilibrium price has no direct connection to shortages and surpluses (choice C). It is also not an agricultural price support (choice D).

(Rigorous) (Skill 22.6)

97. **Capital is:**
    A. Anyone who sells his or her ability to produce goods and services
    B. The ability of an individual to combine the three inputs with his or her own talents to produce a viable good or service
    C. Anything that is manufactured to be used in the production process
    D. The land itself and everything occurring naturally on it

Answer: C. Anything that is manufactured to be used in the production process

Anyone who sells his or her ability to produce goods and services (choice A) is labor, not capital. Combining three inputs with one's own talents to produce a viable good or service (choice B) is related to entrepreneurship. The land (choice D) and what is on it pertains to land.

(Rigorous) (Skill 22.3)

98. **Which of the following countries has historically operated in a market economy?**
    A. Great Britain
    B. Cuba
    C. Yugoslavia
    D. India

Answer: A. Great Britain

A market economy is based on supply and demand and the use of markets. While Great Britain may have socialized medicine, it operates a market economy. Cuba, with its ties to Communism, has a centrally planned economy. Historically, China has had a centrally planned economy but is now moving towards a market economy. Yugoslavia was a market socialist economy, but the country no longer exists; it has been split into Montenegro and Serbia.

(Average) (Skill 19.7)

99. For their research paper on the use of technology in the classroom, students have gathered data that shows a sharp increase in the number of online summer classes over the past five years. What would be the best way for them to depict this information visually?

    A. A line chart
    B. A table
    C. A pie chart
    D. A flow chart

Answer: A. A line chart

A line chart is used to show trends over time and will emphasize the sharp increase. A table is appropriate to show the exact numbers but does not have the same impact as a line chart. Not appropriate are a pie chart that shows the parts of a whole or a flow chart that details processes or procedures.

(Average) (Skill 19.14)

100. An example of something that is not a primary source is:

    A. The published correspondence between Winston Churchill and Franklin D. Roosevelt during World War II
    B. Martin Gilbert's biography of Winston Churchill
    C. The diary of Field Marshal Sir Alan Brooke, the head of the British Army during World War II
    D. Franklin D. Roosevelt's handwritten notes from the World War II era

Answer: B. Martin Gilbert's biography of Winston Churchill

Martin Gilbert's biography of Winston Churchill is a secondary source because it was not written by Churchill himself. The Churchill-Roosevelt correspondence, Brooke's diary, and FDR's handwritten notes are all primary source documents written by actual historical figures.

(Rigorous) (Skill 19.4)

101. Mr. Phillips is creating a unit to study *To Kill a Mockingbird* and wants to familiarize his high school freshmen with the attitudes and issues of the historical period. Which activity would familiarize students with the attitudes and issues of the Depression-era South?

    A. Create a detailed timeline of 15–20 social, cultural, and political events that focus on race relations in the 1930s
    B. Research and report on the life of its author Harper Lee; compare her background with the events in the book
    C. Watch the movie version and note language and dress
    D. Write a research report on the stock market crash of 1929 and its effects

Answer: A. Create a detailed timeline of 15–20 social, cultural, and political events that focus on race relations in the 1930s

By identifying the social, cultural, and political events of the 1930s, students will better understand the attitudes and values of America during the time of the novel. While researching the author's life could add depth to their understanding of the novel, it is unnecessary to the appreciation of the novel by itself. The movie version is an accurate depiction of the novel's setting, but it focuses on the events in the novel, not the external factors that fostered the conflict. The stock market crash and the subsequent Great Depression would be important to note on the timeline but students would be distracted from themes of the book by narrowing their focus to only these two events.

(Rigorous) (Skill 19.12)

102. **Which of the following is NOT an excellent way to teach students about World War II?**

    A. To ask a World War II veteran to visit your class and talk to students about the war

    B. To have students read books on World War II

    C. To have students read primary source materials on World War II, such as the text of the Atlantic Charter

    D. To have students watch the movie *Schindler's List*

Answer: D. To have students watch the movie *Schindler's List*

To have students watch the movie *Schindler's List*, a movie that portrays one small aspect of the Holocaust in which hope for the future was a possibility for a small group of Jews. In actuality, and as a whole, the Holocaust was about the mass murder of millions of people who had no opportunity to hope for a better future. Listening to a World War II veteran speak or reading books and/or primary sources about the war are excellent ways to learn about World War II.

(Average) (Skill 20.23)

103. **What event triggered World War I?**

    A. The fall of the Weimar Republic

    B. The resignation of the czar

    C. The assassination of Austrian Archduke Ferdinand

    D. The assassination of the czar

Answer: C. The assassination of Austrian Archduke Ferdinand

There were regional conflicts and feelings of intense nationalism prior to the outbreak of World War I. The precipitating factor was the assassination of Austrian Archduke Ferdinand and his wife while they were in Sarajevo, Serbia.

(Rigorous) (Skill 22.7)

104. **Which one of the following would NOT be considered a result of World War II?**

    A. Economic depressions and slow resumption of trade and financial aid

    B. Western Europe was no longer the center of world power

    C. The beginnings of new power struggles, not only in Europe but in Asia as well

    D. Territorial and boundary changes for many nations, especially in Europe

Answer: A. Economic depressions and slow resumption of trade and financial aid

Following World War II, the economy was vibrant and flourished from the stimulus of war and the world's increased dependence on U.S. industries. Therefore, World War II didn't result in economic depressions and slow resumption of trade and financial aid. Western Europe was no longer the center of world power. New power struggles arose in Europe and Asia, and many European nations experienced changing territories and boundaries.

SCIENCE

(Easy) (Skill 38.1)

105. **Which of the following layers comprises the earth's plates?**

   A. Mesosphere

   B. Troposphere

   C. Asthensophere

   D. Lithosphere

Answer: D. Lithosphere

The lithosphere is made up of the crust and the upper mantle. The lithosphere "floats" on the asthensophere, causing the plates to move across the earth's surface.

(Rigorous) (Skill 31.2)

106. **What conditions are required to create coarse-grained igneous rocks?**

   A. High temperature and pressure

   B. Slowly cooling magma

   C. Quickly cooling lava

   D. Evaporation and cementation

Answer: B. Slowly cooling magma

Igneous rocks are formed from cooling magma and lava. Lava that cools quickly forms fine-grained or glassy igneous rocks, as crystals do not have a chance to form. Magma that cools slowly forms coarse-grained igneous rocks as the crystals are given time to form.

(Easy) (Skill 39.5)

107. **Which of the following describes the law of superposition?**

   A. The present is the key to the past

   B. The oldest rocks in a rock unit are found on the top of the rock column

   C. The oldest rocks in a rock unit are found on the bottom of the rock column

   D. Faults that cut across rock units are younger than the units they cut across

Answer: C. The oldest rocks in a rock unit are found on the bottom of the rock column

Sediments are deposited and cemented on top of old deposits. Therefore the oldest rocks are at the bottom of a column, and the youngest rocks are at the top of a column.

(Average) (Skill 39.1)

108. **How are igneous, metamorphic, and sedimentary rocks classified?**

   A. The chemical composition of the rocks

   B. When the rocks were formed

   C. How the rocks were formed

   D. The location of the rocks within the Earth's crust

Answer: C. How the rocks were formed

Igneous rocks are the result of cooling molten rock, or magma. Sedimentary rocks are created when small rock particles are cemented together. Metamorphic rocks are igneous rocks, sedimentary rocks, or metamorphic rocks that are transformed by heat and pressure.

(Easy) (Skill 34.1)

109. In which period did land animals first appear?

A. 350 to 135 million years ago

B. Devonian

C. Paleozoic

D. Cretaceous

Answer: B. Devonian

Periods and eras are defined by certain events. The Paleozoic era includes five periods, one of which is the Devonian period. In the Devonian period, insects and amphibians appeared. The Cretaceous period is from 135 million years ago to 65 million years ago.

(Easy) (Skill 37.2)

110. Which era had dinosaurs in it?

A. Cenozoic

B. Mesozoic

C. Triassic

D. Paleozoic

Answer: B. Mesozoic

The Cenozoic era began with the appearance of mammals and birds. Insects appeared on land in the Paleozoic era. The Mesozoic era includes the Cretaceous, Jurassic, and Triassic periods.

(Average) (Skill 41.1)

111. Which of the following objects in the universe is the largest?

A. Pulsars

B. Quasars

C. Black holes

D. Nebulas

Answer: B. Quasars

Pulsars are neutron stars. Black holes are stars that have become so dense that light can't escape from the surface. Quasars appear to be stars but are distant galaxies. Nebulas are clouds of dust and gas that give rise to stars under the force of gravity.

(Average) (Skill 38.4)

112. Why is the northern winter slightly warmer than the southern winter?

A. Because the perihelion occurs in January

B. Because of global warming

C. Because there is more water in the southern hemisphere

D. Because Earth rotates on an axis that is not perpendicular to the plane of rotation

Answer: A. Because the perihelion occurs in January

Choice D explains why there are seasons; that is, why in the northern hemisphere January is colder than July and in the southern hemisphere July is colder than January. However, Earth travels in an elliptical path. It is closer to the sun in January than in July.

(Easy) (Skill 34.4)

113. What are ribosomes?

A. Contain digestive enzymes that break down food

B. Where proteins are synthesized

C. Make ATP

D. Hold stored food

Answer: B. Where proteins are synthesized

Vacuoles store food and pigments and are large in plants. Mitochondria are the organelles that produce ATP for energy. Lysosomes contain digestive enzymes and are found mainly in animals.

(Easy) (Skill 34.5)

114. The role of rough endoplasmic reticulum is:

   A. Metabolic functions
   B. Produce lipids
   C. Produce enzymes
   D. Protein synthesis

Answer: D. Protein synthesis

Rough endoplasmic reticulum (ER) synthesizes proteins such as hormones secreted outside the body. Smooth ER produces lipids. Mitochondria help with metabolic functions and the lysosomes produce enzymes.

(Rigorous) (Skill 35.1)

115. What is the purpose of sexual reproduction?

   A. Produce more organisms
   B. Produce organisms that are genetically diverse
   C. Give organisms the protection of male and female parents
   D. Increase social cooperation between organisms

Answer: B. Produce organisms that are genetically diverse

Single-celled organisms reproduce by cell division and somatic cells in a multicellular organism reproduce the same way (mitosis). The purpose of sex is to produce diverse offspring so that the offspring have a better chance of surviving. In meiosis, the chromosome number is half the number in the parent cell, so that there is genetic diversity when the sex cells recombine.

(Average) (Skill 34.2)

116. In mitotic cell division, at what stage do the chromosomes line up in the cell?

   A. Interphase
   B. Anaphase
   C. Prophase
   D. Metaphase

Answer: D. Metaphase

The interphase is the period before mitosis begins. In the anaphase, the chromosomes are pulled apart. In the prophase, the chromatin condenses to become visible chromosomes.

(Easy) (Skill 36.3)

117. According to natural selection:

   A. Individuals within a population are identical
   B. Those with better traits have less offspring
   C. Successive generations will possess better traits
   D. Single individuals evolve to fit their surroundings

Answer: C. Successive generations will possess better traits

Organisms that possess better traits in order for survival tend to have greater numbers of offspring. These traits get passed down from generation to generation, causing later generations to possess the better traits.

(Easy) (Skill 37.7)
118. **Chemicals released by an organism as way of communicating are called:**
    A. Pheromones
    B. Synapses
    C. Chemoreceptors
    D. Thermoreceptors

Answer: A. Pheromones

Pheromones are released by organisms for communication purposes. Animals may use them to attract a mate or use them as a warning signal.

(Average) (Skill 37.3)
119. **Which of the following is not a kingdom in the classification of living organisms?**
    A. Plants
    B. Fungi
    C. Viruses
    D. Bacteria

Answer: C. Viruses

Viruses do not obtain nutrients from their environment and produce new materials. The other kingdoms are animals and protists. Protists are single-celled organisms with nuclei, and bacteria do not have nuclei.

(Average) (Skill 34.3)
120. **Which property do plants have that fungi do not have?**
    A. Sexual reproduction
    B. Photosynthesis
    C. Digestion
    D. Locomotion

Answer: B. Photosynthesis

Fungi get their nutrients from other organisms by digestion. Locomotion is a characteristic of animals.

(Rigorous) (Skill 35.2)
121. **Which term describes the relationship between barnacles and whales?**
    A. Commensalism
    B. Parasitism
    C. Competition
    D. Mutualism

Answer: A. Commensalism

Barnacles need to attach themselves to a hard surface to survive. They benefit from being attached to whales. If the whales benefited too, the relationship would be mutualism. If the whales were harmed, the barnacles would be parasites. If they ate the same food, there would be competition.

(Average) (Skill 31.1)

122. Which of the following describes the transformation of liquid water to ice?

A. Chemical change

B. Physical change

C. Thermodynamic change

D. Non-chemical molecular change

Answer: B. Physical change

Since heat is taken away, it could be called a thermodynamic change. However, a change in state or phase is considered a physical change. It is more closely related to changing wood into saw dust then burning wood.

(Average) (Skill 32.1)

123. Will Lithium gain or lose an electron when forming an ion? How many electrons will it gain or lose?

A. Gain 1

B. Gain 2

C. Lose 1

D. Lose 2

Answer: C. Lose 1

Lithium will lose 1 electron to form an ion. Lithium has a lone electron in its outer shell. Atoms want to be stable by having their outer shells full. It is easier for lithium to lose 1 electron, thereby knocking off an entire shell, then to gain 7 more electrons to fill its outer shell.

(Rigorous) (Skill 30.4)

124. On which of the following does the force of friction between a metal stool and a wooden floor NOT depend?

A. The speed of the chair

B. Whether the stool has three legs or four

C. The type of metal

D. The smoothness of the floor

Answer: B. Whether the stool has three legs or four

The frictional force depends only on the force between the two surfaces and the nature of the two surfaces. Choice A is wrong because static friction is greater than moving friction. The number of legs determines the area of contact.

(Easy) (Skill 30.1)

125. Which of the following laws implies that the force on an object comes from another object?

A. Newton's first law of motion

B. Newton's second law of motion

C. Newton's third law of motion

D. Coulomb's law

Answer: C. Newton's third law of motion

Newton's second law states the connection between force and acceleration. Newton's first law says if there is no force there will be no acceleration. Coulomb's law and the law of gravity says what the force between two objects will be. Newton's third law says forces come in pairs, which implies that the force comes from another object.

(Easy) (Skill 32.2)

126. Which of the following quantities has the units of calories per degree?

A. Heat capacity

B. Specific heat

C. Heat equivalent

D. Heat transfer

Answer: A. Heat capacity

Heat capacity is how much the temperature of an object will increase when a quantity of heat is added to the object. The specific heat is the heat capacity divided by the mass.

(Easy) (Skill 27.1)

127. A controlled experiment with tomato plants was conducted to see if the amount of water given to the plants affected the number of tomatoes grown. One plant was given 1 gallon of water, another 2 gallons, another 3 gallons, etc. The number of tomatoes produced for each plant was measured. What was the controlled variable?

A. Type of plant

B. Amount of water

C. Number of tomatoes

D. Amount of fertilizer

Answer: A. Type of plant

The amount of water is the independent variable, and the number of tomatoes is the dependent variable. Each time the same type of plant was used, which meant there were only two variables in the experiment. Presumably, the amount of fertilizer was also controlled, but the question did not mention fertilizer.

(Easy) (Skill 25.1)

128. Which of the following should be limited in a balanced diet?

A. Carbohydrates

B. Fats and oils

C. Proteins

D. Vitamins

Answer: B. Fats and oils

Fats and oils should be used in moderation. Saturated fats can lead to heart disease and high cholesterol.

(Average) (Skill 25.1)

129. Which of the following statements about scientific knowledge best explains what scientific knowledge is?

A. Scientific knowledge is based on experiments

B. Science knowledge is empirical

C. Scientific knowledge is tentative

D. Scientific knowledge is based on reason

Answer: B. Science knowledge is empirical

Experiments involve observing two quantities to determine the relationship between them. Observing means gaining knowledge from one of the five senses, which is another word for *empirical knowledge*. Scientific knowledge in some areas is tentative because new and different observations are always possible. Science is based on reason, but so are other types of knowledge.

(Average) (Skill 25.5)

130. **An experiment is performed to determine the effects of acid rain on plant life. Which of the following would be the variable?**

    A. The type of plant

    B. The amount of light

    C. The pH of the water

    D. The amount of water

    Answer: C. The pH of the water

    The variable is the value that is manipulated during the experiment. In order to determine proper cause and effect, the plant type, light, and amount of water should be kept the same for various plants, and the pH of the water should change.

(Average) (Skill 44.1)

131. **Calisthenics develops all of the following health and skill related components of fitness except:**

    A. Muscle strength

    B. Body composition

    C. Power

    D. Agility

    Answer: C. Power

    Calisthenics is a sport that actually helps to keep a body fit in by combining gymnastic and aerobic activities. Calisthenics develop muscle strength and agility and improves body composition. However, calisthenics do not develop power because they do not involve resistance training or explosiveness.

(Easy) (Skill 44.2)

132. **Which of the following should be limited in a balanced diet?**

    A. Carbohydrates

    B. Fats and oils

    C. Proteins

    D. Vitamins

    Answer: A. Carbohydrates

    Carbohydrates are the main source of energy (glucose) in the human diet. The two types of carbohydrates are simple and complex. Complex carbohydrates have greater nutritional value because they take longer to digest, contain dietary fiber, and do not excessively elevate blood sugar levels. Common sources of carbohydrates are fruits, vegetables, grains, dairy products, and legumes.

(Average) (Skill 45.8)

133. **Which type of physical education activity would be most likely to help students develop a sense of belonging?**

    A. Solitary activities

    B. Teamwork activities

    C. Competitive activities

    D. Creative activities

    Answer: B. Teamwork activities

    One of the benefits of participating in physical activities is that students often develop a sense of belonging. This most often occurs in team sports, where students feel a sense of belonging to the team. The relationships developed with others in the process can also create a larger sense of belonging, such as feeling like one belongs to the school community.

(Average) (Skill 45.1)

134. Which of the following help children to develop fine and gross motor skills?

- A. Tearing newspaper into strips
- B. Cutting pictures from magazines
- C. Manipulating play dough
- D. All of the above

Answer: D. All of the above

The above activities will build strength in a child's fingers and hands, which will aid in the development of their writing skills. In order for children to write correctly, they must first develop their fine motor skills. Before being required to manipulate a pencil, children should have dexterity and strength in their fingers, which helps them to gain more control of small muscles.

(Average) (Skill 45.10)

135. Which of the following activities incorporates physical science with physical education?

- A. Analyzing how runners can reduce friction
- B. Studying the use of statistics in sport
- C. Researching how athletes use sports psychology
- D. Considering the biochemistry of producing energy

Answer: A. Analyzing how runners can reduce friction

Physical education can be incorporated with other learning areas, such as physical science, mathematics, natural science, and kinesiology. Analyzing how runners can reduce friction is an example of incorporating physical education with physical science.

(Average) (Skill 45.12)

136. The teaching of sports psychology incorporates physical education with _____.

- A. physical science
- B. natural science
- C. mathematics
- D. social science

Answer: D. social science

Physical education can be incorporated with other learning areas, such as physical science, mathematics, natural science, and kinesiology. Teaching sports psychology is one example of incorporating physical education with social science.

(Easy) (Skill 45.4)

137. Which of the following benefits can physical education provide?

- A. A sense of belonging
- B. Increased self-esteem
- C. Appreciation of beauty
- D. All of the above

Answer: D. All of the above

Physical education provides a wide range of benefits, including physical, emotional, and social benefits. These include a sense of belonging, increased self-esteem, appreciation of beauty, good sportsmanship, increased humanism, valuable social experiences, and improved health.

(Average) (Skill 45.7)

138. **Which locomotor skill is a game of Fox and Hound most likely to be used to develop?**

    A. Creeping

    B. Hopping

    C. Galloping

    D. Leaping

    Answer: C. Galloping

    Galloping is a locomotor skill that involves forward or backward advanced elongation of walking combined and coordinated with a leap. Playing a game of Fox and Hound is one activity that helps develop galloping skills.

(Easy) (Skill 43.2)

139. **Which subject would be most likely to develop a student's body awareness and listening skills?**

    A. Visual arts

    B. Dance

    C. Drama

    D. Music

    Answer: B. Dance

    Younger children learn to develop body awareness through dance. Listening skills are also developed as the students listen to the rhythm of the music and develop a sense of tempo.

(Easy) (Skill 43.1)

140. **Which of the following is considered the universal language?**

    A. Math

    B. History

    C. Music

    D. Art

    Answer: C. Music

    Music is the universal language. Young students enjoy listening to and making their own music. When young children are given the opportunity to learn how to move their bodies through space, they are using body language to communicate their feelings and observations of their inner worlds.

More Study Tools to Help Pass Your Certification Exam

XAMonline.com

Pass your exam with our suite of superior study tools, including:

- Print books
- eBooks
- eFlashcards
- Web-based interactive study guides

Teaching in another state? XAMonline carries 500+ state-specific and PRAXIS study guides covering every test subject nationwide.

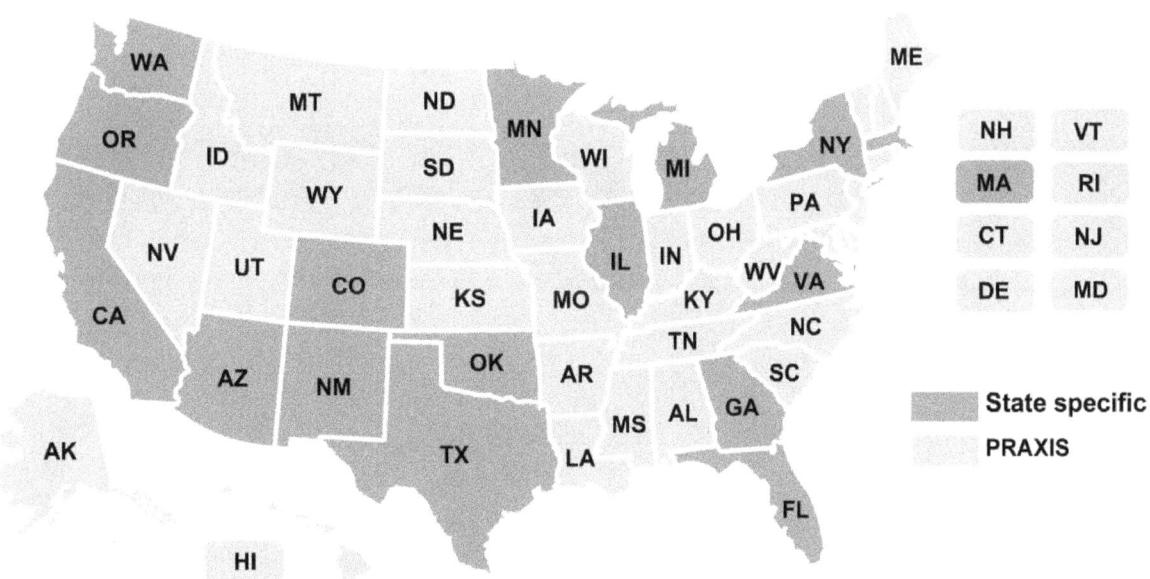

Call or visit us online!
800.301.4647 | www.XAMonline.com